A Living Sacrifice

The Life Story of Pastor Allen Yuan

Lydia Lee

D1374966

Sovereign World

Sovereign World Ltd
PO Box 777
Tonbridge
Kent
TN11 0ZS
England

ISBN 1 85240 293 8

The publishers aim to produce books which will help to extend and
build up the Kingdom of God. We do not necessarily agree with every
view expressed by the author, or with every interpretation of Scripture
expressed. We expect each reader to make his/her judgement in the
light of their own understanding of God's Word and in an attitude of
Christian love and fellowship.

Typeset by CRB Associates, Reepham, Norfolk.
Printed in the UK by Clays Ltd, St Ives plc.

Contents

About the author

Lydia Lee is a journalist and friend of Pastor Allen Yuan. She spent almost a year in China researching this book. During that time she interviewed Pastor Yuan, his wife, co-workers and church members, gathering a great deal of original material and photographs from them. The photographs and much of the information are published here for the first time.

Preface

Yuan XiangChen, better known as Allen Yuan, is a famous leader of the House Church Movement in Mainland China, a man greatly used by the Lord in the twentieth century. He was converted at age eighteen, and since that time he has responded to God's love with his entire life, given to God as a living sacrifice and as a witness for the gospel. He has lived a life of faithful and worthy service to God.

In the course of my acquaintance, conversation and relationship with Mr Yuan, I witnessed how God guided a seemingly insignificant and imperfect life, and how this life glowed because of the presence of God. This glow became a blessing for many Chinese Christians and has also been a great help to me in my own spiritual walk.

Although there are already some testimonies about Mr Yuan's life, I felt burdened to work on a complete biography in order to express my gratitude to the House Church Movement in China and to Mr Yuan. Praise God, when I proposed the idea to Mr Yuan, his family and co-workers, they agreed and supported me unanimously. Mr and Mrs Yuan took me through the whole of their lives, remembering and recording the relevant material. This book is based on first-hand accounts and was read and corrected by them and the other respected elders.

Lydia Lee
Mainland China

Foreword

Of the list of brothers and sisters I have met and ministered to in almost fifty years of serving the Suffering Church, few come higher than Pastor Allen Yuan.

Read this book you must. The detail, which the author goes into to show the suffering and victory in one Chinese family, is absorbing.

I hope like Pastor Allen and with me, you are ready to say to God, 'Take my hand and lead me on.'

Brother Andrew
President Emeritus
Open Doors International

PART I

'You knit me together in my mother's womb'

Chapter 1

Childhood

In 1914 China was at last freed from the grasp of feudalism, and new ideologies and isms were emerging. Since the westernization movement, the nation seemed to be enjoying a boom but in reality it was in a mess with political power struggles the order of the day. This political turmoil would continue until 1949, bringing, on the one hand, years of bloody war, barrenness and much misery, and, on the other, great blessing, as the gospel advanced in unprecedented ways. In 1914, there were more than 30,000 missionaries, and 100,000 believers in China. God had not forgotten the four hundred million people in this land. In this most difficult period in the nation's history the gospel was flourishing.

In 1914, in the sixth month of the lunar calendar, Fenggang in Anhui Province was experiencing one of its hottest summers. The entire city, bathed in bright sunshine, was enveloped in a humid atmosphere and everything was still. At the home of a middle-class family, the atmosphere was even less comfortable: while a midwife and maids hustled and bustled all around, and the husband paced up and down unable to offer any help, a woman agonised in childbirth. After a short while, a baby was born, and the midwife shouted in excitement, 'It's a boy, a boy!' When the man who had been anxiously pacing up and down wringing his hands heard this, he could hardly contain his excitement. Joy and celebration drove out the humid and close atmosphere, and filled the whole house.

Yuan YuTing, the father of the newborn child, came from Dongguan, Guangdong. His father had worked for Mr Yuan TianYou, an engineer engaged on the Jingzhang Railway building project and for this reason the family had moved from Guangdong to Nankou town in Beijing. Yuan YuTing, who had lost both of his parents in his early childhood, had received a western education and had a working knowledge of English. When he had grown up he had followed in his father's footsteps and worked at the Railway Department. As his job as a customs officer involved a lot of travelling, he and his wife later settled down in Fenggang in Anhui Province. He had a regular income and was comparatively well off. As the only son in the family, the responsibility of continuing the family line fell on him, and that was why he was so glad to have a boy as his first child.

His wife, Luo XiaoChun, had a similar family background. Her father had also come from Guangdong and worked in the Accounting Division of the Tianjin Railway Department. Their fathers had been old friends. Luo XiaoChun was also the only child in the family, and was therefore much cherished by her parents. Though she had been born into a rather conservative and backward generation, she had not only never had her feet wrapped, but had also been well educated. She was a graduate from a women teachers' college and was skilful in embroidery. Like her mother, she was a faithful Buddhist and always carried a rosary with her.

Excited about the arrival of their newborn son and full of expectation for him, the couple gave the child Yuan ZhenBang[1] a nickname, A Bang. These were years of much national upheaval and the whole family placed their hope in this little boy to revive the nation's future hopes. In those days this was the noblest ambition any parent could conceive of.

As well as joy, the baby caused a degree of concern to his parents, particularly regarding his health. He had been born prematurely at seven months and was a sickly child who ate little and would always have diarrhoea after meals. As a result, he was very skinny. His mother's health was also not very good and so A Bang was bottle-fed from birth. Because he was so sickly he became the centre of attention for the whole family. Things did not improve as he grew up. A Bang was always smaller than other children and he was slower learning how to walk and talk. His health was always poorer than other children's, despite the fact that he had a good diet. Worried about their child, his parents consulted a fortune-teller who told them that, because of the boy's weak health, they needed, on his behalf, to 'adopt' a foster-mother with a surname that had the meaning of an animal. Otherwise, he would die. It could be any animal, but preferably 'lamb' or 'horse'. Eventually, they found a foster-mother with the surname Yang. Even though it did not mean 'lamb', it sounded like lamb, and they hoped that would be good enough. They hoped their association with her would be auspicious.

When A Bang was one year old, his father was transferred to work in the ticket office in Xuzhou, and so the whole family moved there. The eight-year stay in Xuzhou was to bring the family prosperity on the one hand and misery on the other.

During his career in Xuzhou, Yuan YuTing, then in his early adulthood, was hardworking and energetic. With his good educational background and his keen mind and skill, he was able to acclimatise quickly to his new environment. Later, he found a shortcut to get rich. In those days, two different currencies were in use in China. There was the 'silver' yuan, and a new currency banknote printed by the Bank of China. Although both currencies had the same value, people had no confidence in the new banknote – they feared it might devalue in the uncertain socio-economic situation. As a result, they were exchanging the new currency for 'silver' yuan at the rate of 1.5 to 1 on the black market. Businessmen involved in this exchange soon got very rich. Selling train tickets Yuan YuTing received hundreds of units of currency in both 'silver' yuan and the new currency. Since either one was acceptable, he would exchange all the 'silver' yuan for the new currency before paying the ticket office. The profit he made boosted his monthly income. With the riches he was gradually acquiring, he opened a drinks factory. He began to lead an extravagant life and hired a lot of servants and maids. He even had some reserved seats in the cinema on which his name was inscribed. These were the circumstances in which A Bang grew up. He had almost whatever he wanted and was served like a prince by servants and maids. Attendants were specially assigned to take him to the bath and the theatre, or wherever he wanted to go. This was the most comfortable period of his life. It was also the starting point of his journey in search of the meaning of life.

If only Yuan YuTing had heeded the ancient Chinese proverb warning against unjust gain. It was a case of easy come, easy go. The money came so easily that he spent his days indulging himself in all kinds of vices: drinking, visiting prostitutes and gambling. Although the family was enjoying the benefits of his riches, they were also experiencing the down side. Because of his marital unfaithfulness, his relationship with his wife became very tense, and there were endless quarrels. The same scene would be repeated over and over again: husband and wife shouting at each other, followed by things being thrown around, weeping, door-slamming, and a period of deadly silence. After almost every quarrel, Yuan YuTing would leave the house, and when he came back after a few days, the quarrel would resume. A Bang did not understand why his parents were arguing so much, and whenever he saw them quarrel, he would hide in a corner, cowering and trembling in fear, fighting back his tears. His mother seldom played with him now but left the servants and maids to occupy him. She would spend most of her time playing mah-jong and chanting. As the sole successor to the family line his parents treated him quite well some of the time. His father would take him out to play once in a while, and his mother would also treat him nicely when she felt good. But when they were in a bad mood, he often became the focus for them to vent their anger. Then they would ill-treat him and sometimes beat him. His father would hit him with his fists and his mother would cane him on his bottom when he was sleeping naked in a blanket. In short, he was the victim of their unpredictable whims, which vacillated between indulgence and severity.

When A Bang was seven years old, his father sent him to a private school to receive the most traditional education in China. The teacher was a bearded scholar of the latter Ching Dynasty. In the class, the teacher would sit in the centre, while the children stood in a row and bowed before the sculpture of Confucius, before beginning to recite from all kinds of classical literature. They would win a commendation from the teacher if they recited well, but suffer physical punishment if they did not. Holding a ruler, the teacher would ask the children to come out to the front to recite the text they had learned the day before. Those who could not recite would have to stretch out their palm and receive strokes from the teacher's ruler. Although A Bang was quite good in his studies, occasionally he did suffer this painful punishment which sometimes left a scar on his palm. But the teacher would say, 'You've got to be punished. "Spare the rod and you'll spoil the child." Discipline makes a person useful. This is how a scholar is made.' The most memorable contribution of this teacher was not his beatings, however. It was the name he gave to A Bang on his first day at school: Yuan XiangChen.[2] Although it was pronounced the same as his original name and was similar in meaning, this new name expressed in a more concrete way the idea of reviving the nation: it suggested that A Bang would revive the nation by becoming a prime minister or minister. From that time on 'Yuan XiangChen' became his official name.

In 1923, when Yuan was nine years old, his father was still unrepentant and steeped in his indulgent lifestyle. He had not only spent all his money, but he had also stolen a large amount of public funds. His misdemeanour was later discovered and he was fired. Xuzhou Railway Department gave him two options: he must either repay his debt or go to prison. He had no choice but to sell his drinks factory and all his assets. But all these were not sufficient to repay his debt. Eventually his father-in-law, who was still working at Tianjin Railway Department, offered to help him and paid off his debt; otherwise, he would have been thrown into prison. Having lost all their wealth, the family went to Tianjin to live with Yuan's maternal grandfather.

The eight years spent in Xuzhou were like a nightmare to the Yuans. Though they had awoken from the nightmare, the scars were still there. The relationship of Yuan's parents had been so marred over these eight years that they could no longer feel intimate with each other. Yuan YuTing was totally impoverished. Due to the economic recession and his unclean track record, he could not find a job in Tianjin. Eventually, on the back of his father-in-law's recommendation, he was given work at Jinzhang Railway Department as a telegram officer. Later when civil war erupted, the Jinzhang Railway Department ran into financial crisis and he was forced to find a new job. This time he found work as a ticket collector in a cinema in Donghuamen Street, Beijing. With his income so unstable, Yuan and his mother lived with his grandfather in Tianjin, and the family was separated.

The eight years in Xuzhou were also the crucial period when Yuan's personality was formed. He had a rather paradoxical personality, characteristic of those brought up in an unhappy family – he was cowardly and shy yet having a profound hatred of evil; pampered yet feeling unloved; inhibited yet having a strong personality; careless yet conscientious; innocent yet depressive. He was insecure and had no intimate friends. He grew up with these paradoxes.

The time in Tianjin was a new beginning for him. Because his mother was the only daughter of Mr Luo ZiGang (Yuan's grandfather), Yuan, being an only child, was the apple of his grandpa's eye and he felt warmth and love in his home. He could finally live in a home without quarrelling. This was the most enjoyable period of his childhood.

His grandfather rented a multi-storey house in the ceded territory besides Quanyechang in Tianjin and in those days was considered comparatively well off. He sent Yuan to a modern primary school. Since he had previously studied in a private school, the school work was not very demanding for him. During this period, he made a lot of friends, and was always playing in the street. Sometimes he would sing rhymes together with the other children. Like most of the boys his favourite toy was a knife. He asked his parents for a toy knife, but when they did not give him one, he learned how to make one from his friends. An iron bar would be placed on the railway lines, and when a train came, the wheels would flatten it into the shape of a blade. Once Yuan stole a cute little sword from a friend and hid it in a small box. He kept a lot of toys in this small box – knives, beads and models – but he liked this little sword most of all. However, he could only peep at it when nobody was around, and then he would quickly close the lid so that no one would see it. Once when he wanted to buy some marbles and his mother refused to give him any money, he stole a coin from his grandfather and bought a few for himself. He was very good at playing marbles and he always won. Sometimes he would even win some money, and then he would buy some food. He also stole a towel once. Other than these few little misdeeds, he did not commit any serious offence.

Another place in Tianjin which Yuan enjoyed visiting was the house of a friend of his grandfather, Mr Liang, who also worked at the Railway Department, and was very well off. Yuan always accompanied his grandfather and mother when they visited Mr Liang. Mr Liang's granddaughter, HuiZhen, was five years younger than Yuan. HuiZhen, who was later to play an important part in Yuan's life, was often the target of his teasing and bullying. Being five years younger she took this as fun. His mischief-making often merited discipline but he sought cover from his grandparents and, therefore, received fewer spankings during this period. His family liked to play mah-jong and Yuan would play with them into the night. Life was quite relaxing for him. Games, and a little mischief, were his chief occupations during this period. This was also the time when he could break free from the rules and regulations and the servants and maids that had always restrained him.

Notes

1. ZhenBang literally means 'reviving the nation'.
2. In the Chinese character, this 'Chen' is different from the 'Chen' in his original name.

Chapter 2

In Search of God

After working at Zhenguang Cinema as a ticket collector for some time, Yuan YuTing wrote his own testimonial in English and submitted it to the manager of Huabei Film Company. Realising that Yuan YuTing was actually a very literate person with a working knowledge of English, who was being wasted as a ticket collector, the manager promoted him to the censor board of his company to oversee the censorship of the imported films. After that his income began to improve. In the autumn of 1927, Yuan YuTing brought Yuan to live with him and sent him to a local missionary school run by the YMCA. He chose this school for two reasons. First, it was very close and Yuan only had to walk down through Huadongmen to Jinyu Road to its location in Mida Street. Second, the missionary school taught English from primary school onwards. He wanted Yuan to learn English and receive a good education. His decision had nothing to do with religion. So Yuan left his mother and grandparents and went to be with his father in Beijing to continue his primary education.

As Yuan started primary four at the YMCA school, a new horizon opened up in front of him. Those who enrolled in the school were also required to enrol as members of the YMCA. There were three classes of membership – A, B and C – categorised according to the amount of membership fees. Those who paid more were entitled to more benefits, which were the various amenities of the school, viz. badminton court, shuttlecocks and racquets, swimming pool, etc. There were two things in particular that intrigued Yuan at the school, namely a fair-skinned and blue-eyed blonde who taught him English, and the Bible lesson, which was a compulsory subject. In the Bible class, the teacher would teach Bible verses, some of which the pupils were required to recite. Yuan began to learn about Jesus and to gain some general knowledge about Christianity. Recitation was as easy as ABC for Yuan. He was very interested in learning English and he worked hard under Anna Xiao, an American teacher, beginning with pronunciation and the alphabet. Ms Xiao liked Yuan, whom she found to be an intelligent, obedient and linguistically gifted child, and was pleased when he answered her questions in class. Their relationship began to grow. Yuan did well in all his academic subjects at school. The playfulness and mischief acquired in Tianjin were diminishing gradually as he grew up, and he became a conscientious student. He was good at writing English essays which were always read to the whole class as model essays and put up on the notice board for everyone to admire. Due to his excellent performance in his school work, he was chosen as a class monitor and became a helpful assistant to the teachers.

Later, he had a new Chinese language teacher – Mr Shi TianMin. All teachers like good students, and Mr Shi was no exception; he came to like Yuan very quickly. Yuan carefully observed the teachers he liked. He came to the conclusion that Ms Xiao and Mr Shi were different from all the other teachers. The other teachers were often careless in what they said and did but these two were very kind to students and conducted themselves well. The other teachers would smoke and gossip together after school, but Ms Xiao and Mr Shi would refrain from joining them and would instead work hard preparing their lessons. Sometimes some of the teachers would be very rude to the students, but these two were always kind and gentle. Some of the teachers vented their anger on the students, but they always radiated joy and peace. He sensed that they were different from the others, but he did not know why. At that time Yuan's mother was still living in Tianjin while he lived with his father in a tiny room at the cinema. These two teachers showed concern for this student who could not live with his mother. Yuan often went to Mrs Anna Xiao's house and got to know that she had actually been a missionary until her sending church had discontinued their financial support when she had married a Chinese with the surname Xiao. That was why she had to work as a teacher for a living. She was now commonly known as Mrs Xiao and had two daughters and a son. Due to Yuan's frequent visits to her house, his classmates always teased him and said that he was her foster-son. During this period, Mrs Xiao gave Yuan motherly love and care, and they became good friends. He talked to her about any and everything. She was always sharing the gospel with Yuan and trying to persuade him to believe in Jesus. Yuan did not respond verbally, but in his heart, he had already decided that he would have nothing to do with this western religion other than listen to the Bible lessons at school. 'I must honour my ancestors and make a contribution to my country,' he said.

In the autumn of 1930, he moved up to the YMCA junior middle high school. He had grown very tall as a sixteen-year-old, but was still very skinny. He was a very active youth and did well at his school work as well as sports – ping-pong, the high jump, and ice-skating. He also enjoyed drama and was always involved in the various extra-curricular activities and competitions of the school. He was very mature for his age, and began to think deeply about some of the questions of life, and to be aware of and involved in social and political issues. However, his involvement was still mainly ideological. During the Republic Period, the most popular ideology in China was the three-democracy idea proposed by Dr Sun YatSen. Yuan became an enthusiastic supporter. He deeply admired Dr Sun YatSen and fervently believed that it was only the three-democracy idea that could save China. He began to read the writings of Dr Sun YatSen extensively, namely *The Will and Teachings of the Prime Minister*, *General Outline of Building the Country*, *The Complete Volume of Dr Sun YatSen*, among others. He became extremely well versed in them and even memorised some sections. From the time he accepted this new ideology, he began to look at society and life with a critical and judgemental perspective. He began to despise his name because it carried the connotation of the corrupt latter Ching Dynasty. As part of a new generation, he could no longer accept this name. But, he felt, it might not be very practical to change his name completely – he was too widely known by this name, at home and at church. After much consideration, he changed the Chinese character *chen*, which means 'minister', to a different Chinese character with the same pronunciation, *chen*, which means 'enthusiasm'. With this new name, which he began to use from the age of sixteen onwards, he did away with the corrupt connotation and added a sense of youthful energy. The principal of the YMCA school, Chai BaQuan, was at that time a member of the Nationalist Party. Seeing Yuan's enthusiasm for the three-democracy idea, he encouraged him to join the Nationalist Party, but Yuan refused, feeling he was still too young.

Meanwhile, Mrs Anna Xiao and Mr Shi TianMing continued to share the gospel with Yuan. Mr Shi worked closely with Mr Wang MingDao, who later became a prominent leader of the House Church Movement, and always took Yuan to listen to his preaching. Thus, Yuan first got to know Mr Wang MingDao as far back as 1930. In those days, Mr Wang rented a meeting place. At first, Yuan went reluctantly, just to please his two beloved teachers. He would stand in the back row pitying the many people he saw praying in the front of the church. The preaching sounded ridiculous to him. He was always looking out for weaknesses and loopholes to use to refute those who shared the gospel with him. However, he did admire the eloquence of Mr Wang MingDao, but that was all – his eloquence. He felt nothing but scorn for the content. 'There is no God. However well you argue, there is no God!' However, he always felt very uncomfortable whenever Mr Wang spoke against sin in his sermons. How could he be sinful? He was an innocent young man; he had not committed any serious offence and had never been charged in a court. If everyone was a sinner, why didn't the court indict everyone? He had actually confused crime with sin. After each sermon, Mr Shi and Mrs Xiao would ask him how he felt. He would always shake his head and say, 'There is no God. If you can show me what God looks like, I will believe.' They did not argue with him, instead, they prayed for him.

This hardened sixteen-year-old, like any other young man, was beginning to grope for the meaning of life and had fallen into the maze of adolescent struggles. There were three questions to which he had no answers, despite his extensive reading.

1. He always felt that something was bugging him making him question the meaning of life, even to the extent of feeling suicidal. He tried very hard to look for the source of his problems, but he didn't have a clue. As the only son in the family, he was loved and cherished by his parents; his father had a stable income; he was well fed and well clothed; he had good results and good relationships with classmates and teachers at school: he had no reason to feel this way. Since his father worked in the cinema, he could go there whenever he liked. Life should have been relaxing and wonderful for him, but why was he so depressed? He did not understand. One afternoon, he attempted to commit suicide by electrocuting himself, but suddenly he heard a still small voice saying, 'Yuan, how could you do that and let your parents down?' He stopped. But his depression and pessimism remained unresolved.

2   How could he overcome the temptation of sin, and lead a holy life? He had experienced the grip of the power of sin in his family, and he had seen many youths fall and become polluted. He had a profound hatred of sin, and wanted to live a completely holy life, resisting the evil influences of his society. But he knew that it was unlikely that he would be able to withstand the evil tide of this world alone. How could he lead a holy life? He had been searching, and had been disappointed.

3. What happened after death? Were there ghosts? Were
    there souls? Was death the end of everything?

With these questions in mind, he began his journey in
search of the meaning of life. He started by searching for an
answer from traditional religions. In the early 1930s,
Buddhism and Confucianism were the two most influential
religions in China, and so he began to study them. In spite of
its history of a few millennia and its greater influence in
China, Buddhism did not appeal to him because its pessi-
mistic outlook on life did not fit his ambition of honouring
his ancestors and reviving the nation. Therefore, Buddhism
was not the answer. As for Confucianism, it was concerned
with the ethical issues of the here and now, and, therefore, it
could not answer his questions about life after death. Finally,
Yuan turned to Christianity, which had always been available
to him. The influence exerted over him by the missionary
school and his two teachers had already sowed in him the
seeds of the Christian faith. He acknowledged the superiority
of Christianity in the area of ethics, and its profound philosophy of life. However, as a Chinese, he could never accept
this western religion. But the actual reason behind his rejec-
tion was because he did not yet know God. He still refused to
believe in the existence of God. He stubbornly believed that
the immaterial did not exist, and that as science advanced,
humanity would grow into maturity and grow out of their
need to believe in religion. When this last batch of old
Christians died, there would be no more.

This was a period of constant searching and groping for
Yuan. He was interested in every new idea, but none satisfied
him.

In the winter of 1931, Yuan attended a Christmas banquet
held by the school. The banquet was open to all. After
dinner, every participant held a candlestick in his hand and
joined in singing Christmas carols. Then a Congregationalist
pastor, Rev. Wang, stood in front of the crowd and, without
asking for their consent, administered baptism to everyone
by sprinkling water over them. Yuan was thus baptised, but
without genuine faith.

After a period of intense searching, he had still not found the answer. He was suffering deep agony and depression. The emptiness he felt in his heart was like darkness. He knew that human beings needed a faith, but he had rejected the true faith and was still on a painful search. He was not yet willing to believe in the one true God; he was thirsty but was not yet willing to drink the water of life. Although loved he felt unloved; although he was safe he did not feel secure; although he had every comfort he needed he did not have joy. He knew that he needed to be filled with a higher wisdom, but he was lost. Like all who search for truth, he was treading on a painful path.

Blessed are those who agonise in spirit, for those who seek will find.

PART II

'Apart from you
I have no good thing'

Chapter 3

Grace upon Grace

In 1932, a financial crisis at Tianjin Railway Department provided the impetus for Yuan's grandfather to resign from his job and move with his wife and daughter to Beijing to live with Yuan. The whole family rented a house together at No. 14, Xila Road, Beihe, Donghuamen. The property consisted of two compounds with more than twenty rooms. The family only occupied eight of the rooms and Yuan's mother, a very gifted woman, made a lot of money out of renting out the rest of the rooms.

After the initial joy of reunion, Yuan's mother began to discover that her son had become a withdrawn and depressive young man. Communication between them was difficult and she felt more and more distant from him. Fearing that perhaps it was too late to make up the lost ground she concluded, 'He is a young man now; perhaps he has his own thoughts.' She didn't take the matter too much to heart, though, but continued with her daily routine of chanting Buddhist scripture verses, playing mah-jong and gossiping. Meanwhile, Yuan continued to battle with his internal turmoil. He still maintained a good relationship with Mrs Anna Xiao and Mr Shi TianMing and, ever since the so-called baptism in 1931, had begun to be more serious in his pursuit of God, though he had still not accepted Jesus.

On the night of 29 December 1932, Yuan sat at home alone, doing his homework. Outside the weather was icy cold. At 9.30 p.m., having completed his work, he was still sitting at his desk when suddenly he felt something very powerful touch him, and he had a clear and unmistakable impression in his heart that God existed. There is no psychological or physiological explanation for what happened. He had no idea where the impression came from – but it was very real. Up until that moment he had always been convinced that there was no God, but now, suddenly, he felt the existence of God without any shadow of a doubt. He accepted God and submitted his life in obedience to Him. He blew out the lamp and knelt down to pray: 'O God, forgive me. Now I'm willing to acknowledge your existence and accept you as my Saviour. Please forgive all my sins.' Aware that he had broken the laws of morality and conscience, he confessed all the sins of which he was aware: lying, theft, bullying, hypocrisy, hatred, selfishness, envy, pride, impure thought, etc., and asked for God's forgiveness by Jesus' blood. After he had said the prayer, tears of gratitude ran down his cheeks. As he lay face down on the floor the heavy load he had been carrying disappeared. At last, he was at rest. This historic moment was written in his memory forever. Having received Jesus as his personal Saviour, he had been freed from the bondage of sin. From that moment on he never looked back. He was a new person in Christ. The mental release he experienced lasted forever. As he slowly stood up from the icy-cold floor and lit the lamp, the whole universe seemed to have changed. A whole new world lay ahead of him!

> '... there is rejoicing in the presence of the angels of God over one sinner who repents.' (Luke 15:10)

Yuan never forgot the date of his new birth: 29 December 1932. Due to financial difficulties, he had not celebrated his physical birthday since he was nine years old and he had forgotten the date. Although his mother would sometimes recall how they had celebrated his birthday before that age, with much bustle and excitement, gifts and special food, Yuan had forgotten most of these occasions. He could only remember vaguely that his birthday fell in the sixth month of the lunar calendar and he never actually asked his mother

what the exact date was. But he always remembered the date
of his spiritual birth. He used to say that Christians should
bear in mind that they had been born twice – once physically
and once spiritually. He gave himself the date of birth
recorded on his identity card – 6 June – because he could
remember it easily.

The next day, Yuan told his friends at school about his
experience of being saved through Jesus. When Mrs Xiao and
Mr Shi heard the news, they were overjoyed. He began to
share the gospel with some of his schoolmates, telling them
that it was only through believing in Jesus that people would
find eternal peace and joy. Some of them laughed at him and
said that he had been dreaming, but Yuan did not take it to
heart. He began to take an active part in all kinds of Christian
meetings.

One of the first people with whom he shared the gospel
was his mother's mah-jong partner, Ms Xiang, who came
from Manchuria. Yuan saw her every day when he came
home from school as she came to play mah-jong with his
grandparents and mother. He had already tried to share the
gospel with his grandparents, but they were not interested.
His grandma said, 'You're still young and ignorant, you've
been cheated by foreigners. You'll regret it when you finally
wake up.' But Ms Xiang was different. She was very attentive
to what Yuan had to say and asked a lot of questions.
Yuan kept praying for her. After thinking things through,
she repented and believed in Jesus. After her conversion, she
stopped playing mah-jong with Yuan's family, but instead
talked to him about her new-found faith whenever she came
to the house. Her spiritual life grew rapidly. She attended
Christian meetings frequently, stopped sinning, and shared
the gospel with others. She even had meetings at her home.
Yuan often visited her, and shared God's Word with her.
She was his first-fruit, and a great encouragement to him.
Yuan continued to share the gospel with his neighbours.
Later, a young man about his age, who went on to become a
doctor, was converted. Most of the people with whom he
shared the gospel – except his own family – responded
positively. He always remembered Paul's words, '*Woe to me*

if I do not preach the gospel!' (1 Corinthians 9:16b). Through-out his life it was Yuan's experience that God fulfils His promise, *'Ask and it will be given to you'* (Matthew 7:7). He was like a little child; whatever he asked from his Father was given to him. God's gracious gift of new converts encouraged his at first small faith, and this motivated him further to share the gospel.

Yuan continued to attend Mr Wang MingDao's meeting every Wednesday. He was very earnest in his pursuit of truth and in his study of the Bible. He would seek help from Mr Shi TianMing whenever he had any difficulties in understanding the Bible. He also worked harder to learn English and, in addition to other meetings, attended the English Bible study held at the YMCA. He began to understand the significance of baptism – that it meant dying to the old self, and being buried and resurrected with Christ – and realised that his 'baptism' at the Christmas banquet in 1931 had not been genuine. For one thing he had not then confessed his sins to God and, for another, according to his understanding of the teaching of the Bible, baptism should be by immersion not sprinkling. He talked to Mr Shi about being re-baptised. Mr Shi was very pleased and explained to him more about the meaning of baptism. He told Yuan that Mr Wang MingDao had been fired from his job as a teacher after being baptised by immersion, and that he himself had left the school because of this incident. When he was convinced that Yuan had really understood what baptism meant, he discussed it with Mr Wang. Yuan was baptised in August 1933, along with more than ten other people, at Qing Long Bridge behind Mount WanShou. It was Mr Wang's second baptismal service. On that day, Mr Meng XiangZhao, who later became an elder of the Kuan Street Church, was also baptised. A photograph was taken of the two of them together, on the back of which was written: 'second batch, August 1933.' Mr Wang put those who wished to be baptised through a tough examination. There were many rounds of interviews followed by a period of learning and testing before candidates were considered. He would not consider anyone who was not sure of his or her salvation. He cared about quality, not quantity. Mr Wang's conscientiousness left a strong impression on Yuan's life.

Yuan began to realise that there were some doctrinal problems at the YMCA. Strictly speaking, the YMCA was not a parachurch organisation; it was a civil organisation. The YMCA at his school did not preach the crucified Jesus but emphasised social service, improving society and philanthropy. The YMCA motto was taken from Mark 10:45, *'For even the Son of Man did not come to be served, but to serve...'* However, it left out the second part of the verse, *'... and to give his life as a ransom for many'*, which was the most important reason why Jesus came. In spite of its label 'Christian', it was in reality an organisation propagating a social gospel.

In the autumn of 1933, Yuan went up to senior middle high school, the commerce school run by the YMCA. It was a good school, offering popular courses such as accountancy and typing. In the 1930s, people who had studied these subjects had no difficulty getting jobs in banks. This commerce school had a special attraction: loans were given to poor students, which could be paid off after they had graduated.

The heavy study load at the commerce school did not distract Yuan from his desire to grow in his spiritual life. He continued to attend meetings and to be passionate about sharing the gospel. His life was filled with his first love for Christ, which brought him great joy, but at intervals he experienced great internal turmoil and times of intense reflection. He was always asking himself, 'Yuan, you already belong to Jesus, but why aren't you living a victorious life? Why are you still conceited, proud, jealous and selfish? Why can't you be a perfectly sinless man?' He would recite Romans 7:18–24 ('... the complete verses...') over and over to himself, feeling that Paul vividly expressed his own internal struggle. However, Yuan could not experience the victory Paul expressed in verses 24–25:

> *'... Who will rescue me from this body of death? Thanks be to God – through Jesus Christ our Lord!'* (Romans 7:24–25)

He did not know that he had to depend on the power of the Holy Spirit.

In the winter of 1933, Rev. Wuxi from Shandong Charismatic Church came to Beijing. Due to his extreme charismatic emphasis, churches in Beijing did not dare to invite him to preach, but Mr Cui, the Principal of the YMCA English evening school, did invite him. As Yuan was attending the English Bible study, Mr Cui invited him to the meetings and altogether he attended three meetings. The first two were very chaotic and he was not very impressed. Some were crying, some were laughing, some were speaking in tongues and some were singing in the Spirit. On the third occasion, he went straight from a class and arrived as they were all praying. So he knelt down and joined them. Mr Cui came to him and, laying his hands on his head, prayed, 'Forgive his sins.' No sooner had he spoken these words than Yuan began to sob uncontrollably. He wept loudly, and tears ran down his cheeks. Never in his life had he cried in such a way. After crying he began to laugh uncontrollably. He continued to laugh on the way home on his bicycle after the meeting. That night, Yuan experienced the freedom of victory. He had a good night's sleep, for God had wiped away all his tears.

At that time, Yuan still did not understand many of the Bible's teachings, but after that evening his spiritual life changed. He had been longing for love and now the Spirit of God had poured love upon him – the love of God. The love and the Spirit of God had cleansed him. His heart was filled with gratitude and praise. His initial zeal for the Lord had turned into a deep relationship with God. His spiritual life began to mature. As he continued to study the Bible he discovered in Acts that the work of God was not achieved through might and power, but through the Holy Spirit. In order to be able to rely on the Spirit, one had to be broken and allow the Spirit to take control. The Spirit could only express Himself if He had full control. He understood that a Christian should actively seek to be filled with the Spirit after he had been converted, for this was God's command. As he read church history he saw that the Spirit had enabled believers to survive persecution and to spread the gospel to the entire Roman Empire. He prayed earnestly, 'O God, fill me continuously with Your Spirit. Draw me closer day by day, so that through Your Spirit I may live a victorious life.'

Chapter 4

Calling and Training

In the summer of 1934, Yuan had completed his senior middle year, and was preparing to move up. He was at a very important crossroads in his life. He had received a vision from God which he felt was his life's calling. It was a call to preach the gospel to the unevangelised people of China. It was becoming clearer and clearer, stronger and stronger, until like Paul he experienced the sense of being *'compelled to preach'* (1 Corinthians 9:16) and he knew he needed to respond to God's call. He almost told his parents that he wanted to stop going to school and use his time to spread the gospel, for education only increased secular knowledge but could not save people. On the other hand, he was very aware of his family's expectations for him. Although his parents knew that he had become a Christian, because of the poor communication between them, they did not fully understand his faith. They thought that his youthful zeal was a passing phase which he would one day grow out of. Then he would abandon Christianity. It was their hope that he would secure a high salary job, preferably as a government official, so that he would be in a position to take care of them when they grew old. If he continued his studies at the commerce school and completed his final year, he would gain a certificate which would ensure him a high-paying job that would not require much hard work. Then he would be able to settle down and enjoy life. This was Yuan's dilemma and he often asked himself, 'How should I respond to God's call? Can I pretend I've never heard it? No, I can't!' Again and again he determined to obey God's call rather than his earthly ambitions, but he stopped short of telling his parents. They were too busy chanting and playing mah-jong to be aware of the intense struggle going on inside him. He knew that his parents had already decided on his future and so he found it very difficult to discuss the matter with them. So he kept putting it off, deciding to tackle it again when he had more faith. He just kept praying for the courage to obey God's call instead of his parents' wishes. He also asked for confirmation from the Lord: if it was God's will for him to work full time for Him, he prayed that Mrs Xiao and Mr Shi would support him. When he talked to them they were very positive. This was a great encouragement for Yuan and he wanted to tell his parents as soon as he got home, but when he saw them his courage failed. He was afraid that opposition from his parents would cause conflict at home and, too, that he would not be able to carry his plans through.

So, for two months he was almost torn apart by his dilemma between obeying God's call and his parents. During this period, God continuously guided and strengthened him through His Word. He felt God speaking to him through Luke 14:26 and Matthew 10:37. He said to himself, 'Yuan, these words are spoken to you. Can you love the Lord more than your parents? Are you willing to take up the cross of Christ and follow Him? Are you willing to take the narrow path and give up all hope of fame and prosperity? Are you willing to be misunderstood for what you have chosen? The Lord has spoken to you through His Word, now it is your turn to answer Him. Are you willing to pay the price for the Lord?'

At long last, Yuan plucked up the courage to talk to his parents. After dinner on the day before his school reopened, he told his parents, 'I'm not going to school any more. I've believed in Jesus and I'm going to spread the gospel so that others will also receive this blessing of eternal life.' His parents were stunned. Yuan repeated his words making it clear how determined he was. This time his parents responded furiously. But he remained very firm. He told his parents, 'I've already made up my mind. So don't pay my school fees any more. I won't be going to school even if you insist on paying the school fees.' His father replied, 'Are you mad? What good is it to stop your schooling for your western religion? Can you make a living out of it? Don't ever mention this again. Stop thinking so much and concentrate on your studies, so that you'll get a good job after graduation.' Yuan said, 'I'm not going to school any more. Jesus has shown me how precious the souls of human beings are.' His father said, 'But is there a soul? Can you see it? Is there really such a man called Jesus? Even if He existed, when did He tell you not to go to school any more?' Yuan said, 'God has asked me to offer my body as a living sacrifice, which is pleasing to Him and is my obligation as a believer of Jesus.' His father shouted at him, 'I've raised you for all these years, but you haven't offered anything to me!' and overturned the table angrily. Yuan did not answer back, but went to his room and continued to read the Bible.

The next day, after much deliberation between themselves, his parents changed their harsh tactic to a gentler approach. They had Yuan's grandparents talk to him, for they loved him very much and had a good relationship with him. His grandparents tried to win him over by their tears, but to no avail. Yuan did not argue with them, but he insisted, 'I've made up my mind and I will not regret it.' His grandparents asked him, 'If you stop your schooling, what will you be able to do in the future?' 'Spread the gospel,' Yuan replied. His grandmother said, 'But you can't make a living out of it. You've got to think about your livelihood.' Yuan replied, 'The Lord will provide.'

Then it was his mother's turn to try to persuade him. She took a similar tack to his grandparents: 'You can't make a lot of money out of pastoral ministry. You won't be able to make a living. You're twenty years old now. Are you going to live on your parents for the rest of your life?' Finally, his father toned down his harsh approach and pleaded with him, 'Doesn't it say in one of the Ten Commandments in the

Bible that you should honour your parents? Honouring is obeying. Will you follow the teaching of the Bible and honour your parents by listening to us, just this once?' This was the first time his father had ever spoken to him like this, without his usual harshness, and Yuan almost backed down. But he quickly came to his senses and did not compromise. He listened but he did not answer them back.

His whole family came to the conclusion that he had been brainwashed by western religion, that he was unreasonable, and lacked ambition. They even doubted his sanity. There was, they concluded, no hope for him. But Yuan remained firm in his decision to follow Jesus.

Yuan had taken his first step in his life of ministry. It had not been at all easy for him, but it was an encouraging start. He had never imagined how much painful persecution he would encounter from his own family – as the Bible says, *'a man's enemies are the members of his own household'* (Micah 7:6). His first lesson was learning how to cope with pressure and persecution from his family.

On the basis of the vision given by God, Yuan dropped out of school and prepared to serve the Lord and spread the gospel for the rest of his life. Initially he was not very clear about where God would lead him but, with simple faith, he handed his life and future over to the Lord in prayer. He understood that his immediate concern should be to spend time studying the Word of God in order to equip himself for the future, but he did not know how. Shortly afterwards, God opened a way for him.

The Far East Mission (FEM) began to set up branches of its ministry, the Far East Theological Seminary (FETS), in various cities in China in order to equip Chinese nationals. It had already established branches in Japan and Korea and, beginning in 1930, it began to set up campuses in Guangzhou, Shanghai and Beijing. The FETS Beijing campus was situated at No. 14, Donghuangchenggen, Dianmen. The admission requirements were: completion of junior middle school, assurance of God's calling and being age twenty-two or over. Yuan was then only twenty years old, and therefore his application was rejected. However, the director of admissions advised him to audit some courses, although his young age would mean he would not get a certificate. Yuan told the director, 'In Christian ministry, it doesn't matter if I have a certificate or not, as long as I have the calling of God. I'm called by God, and I have come to the seminary to study God's Word, not for a certificate.'

The course lasted four years, three-and-a-half of which were college-based and the remaining half a year on the field. During the first three-and-a-half years, the students would attend classes in the morning and minister in churches in the afternoon. Auditing students were not required to live on campus as the full-time students were. Accommodation and food were provided free of charge for the full-time students, but the students on audit were not given these benefits. Yuan had to pay a small sum of money for the class notes and this caused some difficulty for him. His dropping out of school had already strained his relationship with his parents and, as he could not support himself but had to live on his parents, it would have been adding insult to injury to ask for money. He prayed repeatedly about this and God spoke to him through a verse in the Bible, *'...believe that you have received it, and it will be yours'* (Mark 11:24). God's work can only be accomplished through faith. If he could not trust God in such a trivial matter, how could he do great things for the Lord? God would not allow His servant to lose his opportunity to study because he could not afford the class notes. So, he continued to concentrate on his studies at FETS.

The three-and-a-half years of study at FETS were a testing time for Yuan, during which he experienced considerable difficulties and suffering. He would wake up at about five o'clock in the morning to have his personal devotions, light a fire after sunrise to heat up the leftovers from dinner the day before for his breakfast, and boil water for his parents. At about seven o'clock, he would go to FETS by bicycle, closing the door very quietly as he left the house so as not to wake his parents. When he came home from school, the family would already have finished their lunch so he had to heat up the leftovers. He would stay at home in the afternoon to go through his class notes and prepare for the next day's lessons. In order to punish his disobedient son, Yuan YuTing had assigned him some house chores and so Yuan had to wipe the three lamp covers every day and open the door for his father every night. Yuan YuTing had been an alcoholic for many years. He would go to the pub after finishing work at the cinema at about eleven o'clock and would come home some time after twelve. When he arrived, he would ring the wind-bells and Yuan would have to get out of his blanket and open the door for him, whatever the season. If he was slow, his father would scold him angrily, 'You're useless. I'd rather breed a dog, at least it watches over the door. You don't even measure up to a dog. You can't even open the door properly. What are you good for?' Yuan would go to sleep at eight o'clock every night so that he could wake up to open the door for his father. But sometimes, he would still wake up late. Nevertheless, he would keep quiet whenever his father scolded him and hold back his tears. His mother's attitude towards him was no better. When she saw that Yuan's clothes were torn, she pretended she had not noticed and did not repair them for him. When winter came, he had no thick shoes and clothes, but he dared not ask his parents. If he were to ask them for money, they would reprimand him for not having continued his education and not earning money. Once, Yuan went with some Christian friends to share the gospel in one of the suburbs of the city. Before he went, he asked for a blanket, but his mother would not allow him to take one out of the house. In tears, he put the blanket down and went without. A year later, his parents adopted a little girl from an orphanage. They would tell their friends, 'I've given birth to a useless son and I've brought him up in vain. Now I'll put all my hope in this daughter. Hopefully she will marry the governor and look after us in our old age.'

God moulded Yuan through his family. Living in this relatively well-off family and yet having to live a life of hardship for the sake of the Lord was an experience which shaped his character and helped him become a more resilient person. As the Scriptures say,

> *'Although the Lord gives you the bread of adversity and the water of affliction, your teachers will be hidden no more; with your own eyes you will see them.'*   (Isaiah 30:20)

In the spring of 1936, Mrs Charlie Cowman, the founder of the Far East Mission, came to the FETS Beijing campus to visit the students. She found out that Yuan loved the Word of God so much that he did not mind auditing the courses without getting a certificate and gave him a signed copy of her book, *A Stream in the Desert*. She liked him and encouraged him to continue his studies.

Meanwhile, Yuan began to get involved in ministry. He became acquainted with a woman by the name of Md Sun Huiqing (Mrs Guo), a member of John Sung's evangelistic association, who often came to attend the meetings held by the FEM. A very zealous Christian from a well-to-do family, she rented a meeting-point at Beixin Bridge and Yuan often preached there. Later, another Mrs Guo began a meeting in a village and invited him over to preach. Yuan began to minister regularly in these two places.

In the same year, Yuan also met Rev. John Pattee, an American missionary from the Nazarene Church who came to Beijing to learn Mandarin. A foreign missionary would normally spend a year learning Mandarin before embarking on ministry. Pattee was a conscientious man with a passion for the lost. He wished he could learn Mandarin quickly so that he could evangelise China. He often taught evening classes held by the FEM, and shared the gospel with the Chinese students who wanted to learn English. Yuan got to know him through these evening classes. Pattee chatted with Yuan a few times and was very impressed with him. He discussed the possibility of evangelising rural areas together once he had mastered the language. But Yuan said, 'The countryside is a vast harvest field for the gospel. I think I'm called to spread the gospel in the rural areas, but not now. The time is not right yet. First I must complete my theological studies.' Pattee was a bit disappointed, but, when Yuan graduated, their friendship exerted a decisive influence over Yuan's future ministry.

In the summer of 1936, Dr John Sung held a second nationwide Bible conference on Gulang Island. This conference, which began on 10 July, was a time of systematic and intensive study of the Bible. Yuan very much wanted to attend but could not afford the travelling costs so he prayed about it. Md Sun Huiqing heard that he wanted to go and after prayer paid his fare. For the first time, Yuan was able to be one of the two thousand people attending the conference at the outstation. For a whole month, Dr Sung led two sessions of Bible study every day, beginning at Genesis and working through to Revelation. Due to the large number of participants, after a short while the well on the island dried up. Over the month, through the constant prayer and intense Bible study, the participants grew tremendously in their spiritual lives. Dr Sung's prayer life and his concern for youth left a deep impression on Yuan. Years later, when Dr John Sung's daughter, Song Tianzhen, recalled this Bible conference, she said that her father had recorded Yuan's name alongside that of the conference in his diary.

In 1937, Yuan began to contribute some articles to *Light in the Darkness*, a magazine published by FEM. He also translated an article on personal evangelism at the back of the *Scofield Reference Bible*, publishing it as *Guidelines for Personal Evangelism*, as well as translating some other Christian literature. This was the beginning of his ministry in Christian literature.

In the autumn of that year, an old friend from Tianjin, who was sitting a college entrance examination, came to Beijing and stayed at Yuan's house for a few days. This was none other than HuiZhen, the little girl with whom Yuan had played in his childhood. Yuan had not been to Tianjin for quite a while since the death of his grandfather. He was very busy with his studies and the work of evangelism and, since his other relatives lived in Beijing, he had no reason to go there. HuiZhen was no longer the little girl whom he had bullied. In the twinkling of an eye she had grown into a very beautiful young woman. She had completed her junior middle education in a missionary school in Tianjin and now, with Japan's invasion of Tianjin leaving the city in chaos, she was planning to move to Beijing to continue her studies. Yuan was no longer a naughty boy; he had become someone who was useful to the Lord. Although HuiZhen only stayed at Yuan's house for two days, leaving as soon as she had taken the examination, her journey proved worthwhile. She accepted the gospel which Yuan shared with her. He told her that it was not enough merely to know the name of Jesus at missionary school; for true faith you had to receive Him into your heart. In the war-ravaged China, he told her, Tianjin was unsafe, but Beijing was no better; true peace came from believing in Jesus. This was how HuiZhen accepted the gospel.

Yuan acquired solid biblical knowledge, especially of the Old Testament, during his studies at FETS. The seminary placed a great deal of emphasis on the four basic doctrines of regeneration, sanctification, healing and the second coming of Christ. These four doctrines can be summarised as follows: after being born again, a Christian must actively pursue holiness, must believe that God still does miracles and heals miraculously, and believe in the second coming of Christ.

The doctrine of miraculous healing had a great impact on Yuan for he had always been very sickly since birth and dose after dose of medicine did not seem to work for him. He believed that God would heal him provided he had faith. Therefore, when he started his theological studies at age twenty, he stopped taking his medication and began to pray for healing. From that time, he rarely fell sick and when he did occasionally, he would refrain from medication and only pray for healing. And God healed him time and again.

While he was at FETS, he often said this prayer: 'O God, speak to me directly from Your Word so that my knowledge of it will not build on others' theological views.' Yuan also exhorted others not to be confused by the many differing viewpoints. Of utmost importance, according to him, was the grace of God, not people's opinions. Yuan was very conscientious and was willing to endure hardship in the course of his studies. As a result, Mr Wu Zhi, the principal of the seminary, liked him very much, and their relationship began to develop.

PART III

'I will serve the Lord'

Chapter 5

Tianjin

In the early part of 1938, Yuan completed his studies at the FETS and began his ministry.

His first placement was at Tianjin Holy Chapel, which had begun as a branch of John Sung's evangelistic association and was led by Mr and Mrs Zhang ZhouXin (Mrs Zhang was also Md Chen ShanLi), who later sold their properties and set up the Tianjin Holy Chapel and the Gospel Chapel in the southern part of Tianjin. Mr Zhang had met Yuan through the evangelistic association and later invited him to join the work at the Gospel Chapel. Yuan moved from Beijing to Tianjin and lived on the premises.

During that period he often visited HuiZhen's house, although he did not see her there. Due to the chaotic situation in the city, HuiZhen's parents had arranged for her and her two sisters to stay at a rented house in the concessions because the Japanese troops were not allowed access there. He heard from HuiZhen's mother that she had changed since she had become a Christian. She often stayed at home to read the Bible and had a better control of her explosive temper. She had even thought of going to theological seminary, but due to the seminary's policy of only admitting auditing students at that time and the unsafe political situation she was not allowed to enrol. Yuan was very happy to hear that HuiZhen had made a steady progress in her faith.

One day HuiZhen's mother told Yuan that someone had tried to arrange a marriage between HuiZhen and the son of the governor of a bank, but when HuiZhen knew that he was not a Christian, she refused even to meet him. This had made her father very angry. Since then, HuiZhen had made it clear to her parents that, according to the Scriptures, believers were not to be unequally yoked with unbelievers and she would only marry a Christian. HuiZhen's mother said to Yuan, 'You see, she is about to turn twenty and she is always attending Christian meetings. But the situation is very unsafe and it will be more and more difficult for her to get married as she gets older. She says she will only marry a Christian and she is rather stubborn. Yuan, you are also a Christian. Can you do us a favour and introduce us to a good Christian for HuiZhen?'

Yuan agreed. No sooner had he returned to his dorm in the Tianjin Gospel Chapel than he wrote a letter to his father. This was what he wrote in the letter: 'HuiZhen's mother asked me to look for a husband for her. Actually, I like her very much. If you think that she is suitable for me, would you please write a letter to her parents and ask them?' Yuan YuTing was very glad to receive Yuan's letter and he felt that his proposal to HuiZhen was the only thing he did well over those years. Yuan's grandmother had been severely ill, but when she heard the news, she was so happy that she recovered from her illness and was soon up and about again. Though the Yuans did not match the Liangs (HuiZhen's family) in socio-economic status, they decided to try anyway. Yuan YuTing wrote a long letter to HuiZhen's father. In summary, he wrote: 'I have been told that your daughter HuiZhen has become a Christian and will only marry a Christian. We were very glad to hear that. Our Yuan is also a Christian. If you have no objections, please inform your daughter that Yuan would like to marry her. We know that he could not match HuiZhen in every aspect, but we would be grateful if you would try to persuade your daughter.'

HuiZhen's father was faced with a dilemma when he read the letter. He knew that Yuan was a nice young man who neither smoked nor drank and was an upright person, but he was too poor to be his son-in-law. He did not want his daughter to have to suffer hardship with him. After much consideration, he handed the letter to HuiZhen and left the decision to her. But he warned her repeatedly, 'You'd better think very carefully. In spite of his good character, Yuan is too poor. He doesn't own a house, or land. Being a pastor, he won't make a lot of money. You must think seriously about your future livelihood. Don't rush into a hasty decision.' She gave the proposal a great deal of thought and finally accepted it on the basis that he was a pastor. They were officially engaged in May 1938 and the wedding was held on 22 July 1938.

Although HuiZhen was Yuan's childhood sweetheart and there was no matchmaker, they did not, strictly speaking, experience free courtship. In fact, they never dated each other. Two days before their wedding, HuiZhen arrived in Beijing by train with her mother and sister, and booked into a hotel. It had been raining for the two weeks before the wedding and her mother believed that it would be an ominous sign if it were raining on the wedding day. But, against all expectations, the sun shone brightly. The wedding, which was held in a restaurant in Wangfu Street, combined a mixture of Chinese and Western culture. The couple sat on a Chinese cart, but wore western wedding costumes. The Yuans had invited more than a hundred guests to the wedding ceremony and banquet. Half of the guests were non-Christians, and there were also some foreign pastors among them. The banquet was held immediately after the wedding ceremony. Before the food was served to the guests, according to Chinese custom the bridegroom and bride were served a bowl of noodles respectively. A waiter said to them, 'A bowl of noodles to bring long life to the groom and to the bride. May your marriage last forever.' After the marriage wish, the waiter placed the two bowls of noodles before them. Yuan reacted furiously and said, 'I'm a Christian. I don't believe in this nonsense.' No sooner had he finished speaking than he hurled the two bowls of noodles onto the floor. His mother was very angry at his behaviour but, not wanting to lose face, did not say a word. However, her face looked like thunder for quite a while. Yuan acted as if nothing had happened. This incident left a deep impression on HuiZhen, for this was the first time she had seen her husband angry.

After the wedding, Yuan's mother said to HuiZhen, 'Yuan is quick-tempered and he says whatever he thinks, without much consideration. You must bear with him.' HuiZhen reflected: 'This is the temperament of a true Israelite.' Shortly afterwards, Yuan returned to Tianjin with HuiZhen and continued his ministry there. They stayed with HuiZhen's family for about half a month before they moved to a small house behind the new church to which Yuan had been transferred at Gegu, Tianjin.

Japanese soldiers attended this small church in Gegu, but there was very little trouble. Once, two Japanese soldiers came in and, putting down their guns, they took a piece of chalk and wrote on the blackboard four Chinese characters: war crime. They told Yuan that they were Christians and had been conscripted against their will. All God's children hate war.

Chapter 6

Beijing

Yuan ministered in Tianjin for one-and-a-half years before returning to Beijing in the autumn of 1939, when his wife was about to give birth to their first child. It was a difficult time for Yuan for, on the one hand, he had to take care of his parents and, on the other hand, he was about to assume the responsibilities of parenthood himself.

Meanwhile, Mr Wu Zhi, the principal of the FETS, invited him to take on the job of translator at the seminary. The work was part time – half of the daily office hours – and so he could still continue with his church work. He received a regular monthly salary and, after deducting his monthly tithe and food bill, he still had half of the amount left, which was considered a rather good income at the time. In the latter part of December 1939, Liang HuiZhen gave birth to a son by the name of Yuan FuYin (Fu Yin means gospel) at the Xiehe Hospital. The whole family, especially Yuan YuTing, was overjoyed by the arrival of the baby. He hoped that Yuan and his wife would give birth to five boys and three girls, and he chose the third character of the names for them in advance: Yin, Sheng, Yue, Qing, and Rong. When he gave the names, he had no religious connotation in mind, but Yuan neatly matched it with the second character, Fu, which as a whole gave the name the meaning 'gospel'. Yuan and HuiZhen had two other sons by the names of FuSheng and FuLe.

Yuan worked at the FETS with his normal conscientiousness, never arriving late or leaving early. His main job was to interpret for Mr Wu Zhi when he lectured, but he also translated his class notes into English. His income was regular and life was stable, and he grew richer and richer. Everything was going so smoothly that he began to feel uneasy, and he prayed, 'O God, have I forgotten Your calling in the midst of my plain-sailing life? You called me to save the souls of the villagers, but I'm living such a comfortable life that I feel more and more remote from them. That was the reason I went to the seminary, but my comfortable life has drawn me away from Your calling. O God, if it is Your will for me to go to the village, would You guide me? I'm willing to obey You.'

In the summer of 1940, Yuan met Rev. John Pattee again. He had stopped over in Beijing on his way to Beidai for a holiday. He did not contact Yuan in advance, but they bumped into each other at a FEM church. Yuan believed that this was the providence of God for their chance meeting happened at the very time that he was looking for a way to begin a ministry in the countryside. Rev. John Pattee had just begun to work in the villages of Hebei and Shandong, and was in need of co-workers. They talked to each other about this and God worked providentially to bring Yuan, his wife and his baby to work with Rev. Pattee in the villages in the southern part of Hebei. His parents were very unhappy about Yuan's decision. They thought that it was very unreasonable of him to give up his comfortable urban life in Beijing and go to live in a village. But Yuan was very firm in his decision, certain that it was the leading of God, which he could not resist.

Chapter 7

Ministry in the Villages of Hebei and Shandong

In the summer of 1940, Yuan moved with his wife and son to the eastern part of Cheng'an district in the southern part of Hebei province, and settled into a church there. The living standards in this region were much lower than in Beijing and the villagers' diet consisted of porridge, *wowotou*,[1] sour cabbage, and sometimes carrot. Due to a poor harvest soon after their arrival, from the autumn of 1940 to the summer of 1941, *wowotou* was the only food available. *Wowotou* was made from cottonseeds and corn, and cotton grew abundantly in the south of Hebei. Even the Chinese found it unpalatable, let alone the Americans who usually ate bread and drank milk. But Pattee seemed to enjoy it, and none of them grumbled. Although the natural harvest was poor, the spiritual harvest was rich and they found many people hungering and thirsting for truth.

Each day Yuan, Pattee and a co-worker by the name of Shang ZhiRong would go out to the villages to spread the gospel, while HuiZhen and Mrs Pattee would teach in the school run by the church. While her son FuYin was cared for by a childminder, HuiZhen taught the children in primary six. After classes she had to prepare for lessons and do laundry, as well as supervising the students' homework in the evenings. Though it was very tiring, she enjoyed her work.

The ministry of evangelism in the villages was very tough. When Yuan, Pattee and Shang ZhiRong arrived in a village the first thing they did was put up a tent. They would all wear black Chinese robes and strap a lamp onto their head for light (there was no electricity then). Shang ZhiRong would play an accordion and Yuan a drum. As a prelude to their sharing of the gospel message they would sing hymns. Then all three of them would take turns speaking and, while one was speaking, the other two would pray. When there was a temple celebration, all the villagers flocked to the temple and this was an excellent opportunity to share the gospel. Hearing the drumbeats, people would begin to gather around them. Having a westerner – Rev. Pattee – on the team was also a great draw. When they had gathered a crowd, they would start preaching and sometimes each of them spoke two or three times. The messages were very simple. During the Japanese occupation, people were longing for peace, internal as well as external, and were very receptive to the gospel. Whenever they preached someone was always converted. They would ask those who indicated repentance to stay on for counselling. After speaking to them under a tree or besides their tent, they would lead them in the sinner's prayer. The evangelists worked late and their food was very simple. They would stay in a village for four to five days before going on to continue their itinerant music and preaching evangelism in another village. They would cover about five to six villages each trip, which lasted about a month. The first thing they did after they arrived home was take a bath and soak their clothes in hot water. In the villages hygiene was poor and when they returned home they were infested with lice. After resting for a few days, they would set off on another trip. In about a year, they had managed to cover all the villages in the southern part of Hebei, bringing the gospel of Christ to one village after another.

In their tent in the wilderness, the three servants of the Lord from different racial, linguistic and geographical backgrounds were united together in prayer for their ministry. This was what carried them through many hardworking days and sleepless nights. Though a foreigner, Rev. Pattee had a deep compassion for the lost, often praying and weeping for the salvation of the Chinese right through the night. His zeal and passion touched and inspired Yuan and HuiZhen deeply, and through his life they saw God's great delight in His children's passion for the lost. They also learnt from Rev. Pattee that God's work was done not by might, nor by power, but by His Spirit. The most important qualification of a servant of God was not having the right certificates or eloquent words: it was a passion for the lost. The wilderness was where God trained His servants – Moses in the wilderness of Midian, and David as a shepherd in the wilderness. The wilderness was the best place for servants of the Lord to be educated and to become useful. In the wilderness of these villages, Yuan learnt something he could not have learnt in a classroom. This was where he integrated theoretical knowledge with practical ministry. As he ministered to the people, God ministered to him.

'I'm closer to God out here,' Yuan told Rev. Pattee, who was both his teacher and friend. He had found an avenue to evangelise China: by evangelising the villages, where 80 per cent of the total population lived. Such an endeavour needed a pure heart and a passion for the lost.

From the summer of 1940 to the latter part of 1941, Yuan spread the gospel in Cheng'an, Yongnian, Guangping, Weixian and other areas in the southern part of Hebei province. After that, he went on to all the villages in the five districts in nearby Shandong province. As he had covered these ten districts, he had not only become acclimatised to life in the countryside, but had also discovered the secrets of the effective evangelisation of the villagers: since they had little or no education it was important to use simple jargon-free language; and it was also vital to find contact points with their everyday lives and show them that they could experience God's love in the midst of their daily concerns and difficulties. War had brought much misery, but it had also created precious opportunities for spreading the gospel. Through war people began to cherish the preciousness of peace, and through heartache they came to know what it truly meant to be blessed. Over the one-and-a-half years of their ministry together, the three men had seen many people come to know the Lord, and the number was increasing.

Early in December 1941, Yuan had gone to work in Zao City and the surrounding area of Shandong while Rev. Pattee stayed behind to continue the ministry in the Cheng'an District. On 7 December 1941, the Japanese launched the sneak attack on the military base in Pearl Harbour which resulted in the USA declaring war on Japan. At the time, the Japanese had occupied almost all the territory in the northern part of China and, on that day, they launched their attack on the Americans in China, sending them to the concentration camp in Wei District in Shandong. The Pattees were among them. The Japanese came from the city in a jeep, broke into the church and took them away with their belongings. The Chinese troops collaborating with the Japanese broke into the Yuans' house and looted all their valuables. The Japanese soldiers were badly in need of clothes for the winter, so they took away all their woollen sweaters, trousers and leather shoes. They also stole Yuan's watch from his desk.

At the time, HuiZhen, who stayed behind in Cheng'an while Yuan travelled, was only twenty-two years old. Just before the soldiers arrived, a worker taking care of the maintenance of the church warned her that the Japanese had blockaded the city's entrance, and could arrive at any moment. He said to her, 'You're still so young and, with your husband away, you've got to take care of your child. The Japanese are looking everywhere for young women. You'd better find a place to hide.' HuiZhen put some coal dust on her face and hid in a cellar with her son. No sooner had they gone into the cellar than the Japanese arrived. She was desperately praying that FuYin would not cry, otherwise they would be found. After the soldiers had captured the Pattees and looted the church, they left, telling the gatekeeper that they would be back. They returned shortly afterwards to post some armed sentries to signal that the Japanese had taken over the church from the Americans.

The church was in a mess. With the capture of the Pattees, the preachers and co-workers in the church were very

depressed and did not know what to do. They advised
HuiZhen to stay in the cellar with FuYin for a few days
because the Japanese troops were still there. The preachers
brought meals into them. She was worried about the situation in Shandong and Yuan's safety. Thanks to God, the
Japanese did not create any further trouble. The people in the
church did not know whether to stay or to leave. All they
could do was pray earnestly to God.

Yuan had a similar experience in Shandong. The Japanese
there were not, however, as crude as those in Cheng'an.
He had gone to preach the gospel in the Fan District in
Shandong, adjacent to Cheng'an, and was staying in a small
church belonging to the Xuansheng mission. The Japanese
came by night. Bringing with them an interpreter, they woke
up all the pastors and informed them that they had taken
over. Things belonging to Chinese could be taken away, but
things belonging to Americans must remain. On hearing
this, Yuan assumed that the church in Cheng'an had already
been captured by the Japanese and was anxious about the
safety of his wife and child, and his co-workers, especially
the Pattees. The next day, he left for home. Everyone who
entered the city was examined thoroughly by the armed
sentries and was required to bow to them. Although there
was no trouble, Yuan did not feel comfortable bowing to the
Japanese, and from then on avoided having to use the city
gate.

On arriving at the Cheng'an church, he knew that the
Pattees must already have been captured by the Japanese, but
he could not imagine what had happened to the other
co-workers inside the church. He went round the church,
hoping to meet someone coming out of the building, so that
he could find out what was going on; he did not dare to go
in. After waiting in vain for quite a while, he went to a
secluded place and took off his long-sleeved shirt and his cap
and disguised himself as a peasant. Then he rode a bicycle up
to the church gate, and spoke to one of the sentries. The
Japanese soldier could not understand him and asked him to
speak through his interpreter. Yuan said, 'I'm Chinese. I'm
the pastor of this church. There are some other Chinese in

the church. I need to talk to them and I need to arrange for my family members to go home.' The interpreter was from the North-east, and was a reasonable man. He talked to the sentry and persuaded him to allow Yuan access to the church. When he entered everyone was overjoyed and gathered round him. Seeing his wife with her face soiled with coal dust, and his son sleeping soundly in her arms, he could not stop praising and thanking God. His co-workers told him that the Pattees might have been taken to the concentration camp in the Wei District in Shandong Province, but this was not confirmed. All they could do was pray for them. They then discussed the evacuation of those left at the church. Yuan said that those who wanted to go home, especially those from a distance, could use the money left in the church to get back. Most of them wanted to go home and look for new areas of ministry. Although there was not enough money left for everyone's fares, no one uttered a word of complaint. A local brother, Shang QingMei, noticed that Yuan did not take any money and thought it was because he did not want to deprive others of their fare. After everyone had left, he gave him five Japanese yen and said to him, 'You come from a long way away and have a family to take care of. I'm sure you need this five yen.' Yuan said, 'I'm not going home. I will stay back and continue to spread the gospel here.' Shang QingMei was very surprised to hear this. He thought that since Yuan had followed the American to the area, he would leave if Rev. Pattee were no longer here. But Yuan did not follow man; he followed God and obeyed his call. Wherever Rev. Pattee was, he would continue to stay in the village. He told the puzzled QingMei, 'I'm really not going home. The field is ripe for harvest. We've worked so hard and it's beginning to yield some fruit, how can I leave now?' Shang QingMei was very touched by Yuan's determination to serve the Lord and said to him, 'Since you've decided not to go home, and now that the church has been taken over by the Japanese, why don't you stay at my place? We can work together.' The next day, QingMei brought a bull cart to take Yuan and his family to his house. Shang QingMei lived in North Shanhu village, four kilometres away from the

Cheng'an county town. The Yuans were put up in a small room in QingMei's house. From then on, they lived and ate together with the peasants and became identified with them. HuiZhen gave birth to a baby girl (their second child) in March 1942. She was named Yuan AnHu. The name derived from the place where they were staying – North Shan*hu*, Cheng'*an*. Her name always brought back many memories for the Yuans. Many years later, whenever it was mentioned, Yuan would tell some stories about the friendliness of their neighbours in North Shanhu.

In the spring of 1942, Yuan started a home meeting-point in North Shanhu, Cheng'an County, Hebei. Since the church in Cheng'an had been taken over by the Japanese, and they could not afford to build a church in the village, they had to start a house church in order to meet the pastoral needs of the believers. After dinner almost every evening, Yuan's house would be filled with people. The meetings began with singing led by HuiZhen and since most of the villagers were illiterate, she would teach them the songs sentence by sentence. After the singing, Yuan would preach. Sometimes, he led Bible studies. The neighbours liked to visit this simple house, and they enjoyed playing with Yuan's two children. Sometimes, they would seek his help when they had problems, and, in return, they would always give a hand whenever Yuan and his wife encountered any difficulties. HuiZhen also held literacy classes for the women, teaching them how to read the Bible. The neighbours always commented that HuiZhen was a virtuous and able woman. When she heard this, she would say, 'Actually I don't know anything. I'm just learning from you. You've taught me a lot of wisdom for everyday life.' What HuiZhen said was true. Having been brought up in a rich family, she had been pampered. But now, through the hardships in the village, she had become an able woman. On the third day after she had given birth to her baby girl, Yuan went out to spread the gospel, so she made the fire and prepared meals on her own.

Like all the other women in the southern part of Hebei, she woke up at five o'clock in the morning and went to the sorghum field to collect leaves which were used to make the fire to cook and to heat up the room. She would pick the outermost leaves of the sorghum plants and dry them. Being petite she could not reach the leaves without standing on tiptoes. After she had carefully picked the leaves, moving from one plant to the next, she carried them to the ridge of the field, where she tied them up in a bundle before carrying them home. Once home she laid them out to dry. She had to walk the 2.5 kilometres to the sorghum plantation two or three times a day. When she came back, with her hair and clothes wet from the morning dew, she no longer looked like a pampered girl; she looked like a farmer coming out of a pond. As she cared for her family and fulfilled the tasks of daily living, she was growing in her spiritual life and was being moulded. Due to long-term overwork and extreme fatigue, she was not in good health. Carrying those heavy and wet sorghum leaves over a long time caused her right shoulder to become deformed and she developed a slight hunchback.

In the autumn of 1942, Yuan received a telegram from his mother, informing him that his father had been taken ill with terminal tuberculosis and wanted him and his family to go home immediately. As soon as he read the letter he decided with HuiZhen to take their daughter, AnHu, with them to Beijing to visit her grandfather, leaving FuYin in the care of neighbours. He made this decision because his father had met FuYin, but not AnHu. Yuan was also hoping that, as his father was only fifty years old, he might still recover from his serious illness. In that case they would soon to be able to return to the village and they wanted to spare themselves the trouble of taking two young children with them. So, they only took AnHu.

Due to his unhealthy lifestyle and his long-term alcohol-ism, they arrived to discover that Yuan YuTing was already in the terminal stages of illness. At that time, there was no effective treatment for tuberculosis. The doctor told them to take care of him and give him whatever he wanted to eat, implying that there was only a slim chance of recovery. Yuan YuTing was very comforted when he saw that Yuan's family was in good shape, especially his granddaughter, AnHu. Yuan and his wife shared the gospel with him, and, as he had difficulty speaking, he nodded his head. After being home for more than a month, the church in Hebei sent Yuan a letter, urging him to return to his work. After discussion with his parents and wife, he decided to leave his wife and daughter with his parents while he returned to the church to settle some work before coming back again. He did not know that it would be his last meeting with his father. A few days after he left, his father died. HuiZhen lovingly cared for Yuan's father on his sickbed, sharing the gospel with him right to his last breath. After the burial, HuiZhen returned with Anhu to the village.

Yuan rode on an old bicycle from village to village in the Guangping and Wei Districts, visiting the believers house by house. He showed extra interest in potential host families for the meeting-points. Gradually new meeting-points began to spring up in the Guangping and Wei Districts, led by Yuan. At that time, Mr Shang and his son were his best partners. Together Shang ZhiRong and he cruised around the villages spreading the gospel.

Yuan did not have any interest in politics. Throughout the Japanese occupation, he knew that his job was to spread the gospel and, as long as the circumstances allowed, he was determined he would not stop working. Many people advised him, 'In such a chaotic time, life in the countryside is difficult. Why don't you return to Beijing and look for a job and live a stable life? You can still serve the Lord part time.' But Yuan would reply, 'Spreading the gospel is the only thing I can do. In such a chaotic situation, the gospel is needed all the more. I'm a minister of the gospel, I'm only interested in spreading the gospel.'

A few times on his journeys, he was stopped by Japanese soldiers, but the Lord protected him each time. When the soldiers found out that he was spreading the gospel, they did not create any trouble for him. At that time, the southern part of Hebei was controlled by Japanese troops by day and the Eight-Path Army by night. Yuan and Shang ZhiRong would take both Japanese currency and the currency acceptable to the Eight-Path Army with them on their journeys. If they had only the latter and were to meet the Japanese, they would be mistaken as members of the Eight-Path Army. This would cause trouble and hinder their work of spreading of the gospel. If they had only the former and met the Eight-Path Army, they would be mistaken as Chinese traitors, which would be equally troublesome. Therefore, they had to carry both kinds of currencies in order to support their claim with whomever they met that they were only spreading the gospel. They seldom encountered any trouble.

Once, when he was out with Shang ZhiRong, they suddenly heard the sound of shooting. They quickly jumped off their bicycles and threw away all their money and walked on. They did not know who was ahead of them and what currency they would need to show, and so they thought the best thing to do was simply to throw away all their money to avoid any trouble. On approaching the strangers, they discovered that they were members of the Eight-Path Army. After hearing that they had thrown away their money, the army sympathised with them and invited them over to their camp on the mountain and treated them to breakfast. Yuan and Shang then saw first hand how difficult army life was. Their breakfast was millet porridge. A man who was addressed as Commander Guo, ate with them. After breakfast, the commander sent some soldiers to accompany them down the mountain and told them to be extra careful on the road.

From the time Yuan moved his church from Cheng'an District to North Shanhu village, he seldom entered the city. There were two reasons for this. Firstly, Japanese sentries guarded the city gate and those who entered the city were required to bow to them, something Yuan was not willing to do. So, he only entered the city if it was absolutely necessary for his ministry. Yuan entered into a lot of correspondence, and the second reason was an incident which occurred on a visit to the post office in the city. A Christian post-office worker nervously took him to one side and told him, 'I discovered a lot of anti-Japanese leaflets printed by the Eight-Path Army in your letter. If others were to discover it and told the Japanese, you'd be in trouble.' Yuan looked at the letter and the address of the sender, but had no idea who it was. He was named as the addressee. The post-office worker advised him not to come to the post office himself, because the Japanese were actively searching for anti-Japanese material, and offered instead to send someone to bring his letters to him. Yuan agreed and avoided entering the city from then on. He was also extremely busy, devoting as much time as possible to teaching the villagers, most of whom were illiterate, biblical truth. Due to the inconvenient transportation system at that time, he spent twenty days out of each month travelling around the meeting-points in the various villages. The family was left in the sole charge of HuiZhen.

The number of believers was increasing at the meeting-point he had started in North Gao village, Wei District. The believers were not highly educated, but they thirsted for the Word of God. Every time he went there he would stay for a few days and, when he had to leave, they would urge him to stay longer on his next visit, for they had a lot of questions to ask him. Each time when he came back from the meeting-point, he would say thankfully to God, 'O God, the village is my best seminary. The zeal of the believers often contrasts with my shortcomings towards You.' Gradually, the work in Wei District became the main thrust of his ministry. Some of the most committed believers prepared somewhere for them to live, and the Yuans moved to North Gao village in the Wei District in the autumn of 1944. Their third child, FuSheng, was born there.

North Gao village was a small village surrounded by beautiful countryside with a small river – the Zhang River – beside the village. During the spring every year, the Zhang River would flood the land and then recede. After this the farmers would begin to plough the land and plant the crops. Yuan worked with the farmers every day. He could not do the more skilled farm work well, so he only ploughed the land, but he began to experience the truth of Jesus' words, *'No-one who puts his hand to the plough and looks back ... '* (Luke 9:62). He saw how the farmers sowed, watered and took care of the crops on the farm, and how the crops gradually ripened for harvest, from the little sprout in the beginning to the ripe harvest that covered the entire farmland. As the Bible says, *'Those who sow in tears will reap with songs of joy'* (Psalm 126:5). The field is ripe for harvest! Jesus explained the complicated process of spiritual growth by using a very succinct metaphor,

> *'The harvest is plentiful but the workers are few. Ask the Lord of harvest, therefore, to send out workers into his harvest field.'* (Luke 10:2)

Yuan realised that the growth of the crops resembled the growth of believers' spiritual lives. Only the Creator of heaven and earth could reveal the mystery of the relation- ship of all these phenomena. It suddenly dawned on Yuan that the universe was in existence to manifest the existence of God. In the secluded village, God spoke to His servant and trained him through His creation. The shade under the trees and the field were the best meeting-points. The believers worshipped the Lord by singing hymns as they ploughed the land. Yuan mingled with them, helping them to weed their crops, feed their cattle, and take those who fell ill to the hospital in Xingtai. Like the farmers, he planted all sorts of crops and ate simple food. He was no longer the Mr Yuan who wore a long-sleeved robe and a cap, but he was a trusted brother. Even the traditional women who wrapped their feet could talk to him. They addressed him as father of FuYin.[2]

HuiZhen taught at a school in North Gao. It was a small school attended by only a few pupils. She taught them language and art, and shared the gospel with them. Those simple and innocent children all loved her, especially when she sang hymns to them.

In 1996, some believers from Beijing went to spread the gospel in North Gao. They met an old woman there who asked them if they knew Mr and Mrs Yuan. They said they did. The old woman told them that it was Yuan who had led her whole family to Christ, and she could still remember that Mrs Yuan had taught them singing.

From 1942 to June 1945, Yuan's ministry in the village grew until it reached the stage of maturity. He had received and obeyed the vision from God. He had found a God-given method of evangelism: relying not on any organisation, or any power, but solely on God and living only for the gospel. This was a period of great difficulty for the Chinese. Inflicted with both internal problems and external threats, they were struggling for survival. But the faithful God took care of His servants. Those who trusted in the Lord would not be in want.

When he was ministering in the villages, due to his busy schedule, apart from visiting his terminally-ill father in 1942 for a month, he did not go home. As the only son, he was absent when his father passed away. After his father's death, his mother and grandmother had to live an austere life on their savings. Yuan missed them a great deal, particularly during festive seasons. However, more than anything else, he was grieved by their unwillingness to accept Jesus as their Saviour. As a preacher of the gospel, he converted others and saved their souls, but members of his own family were heading towards eternal destruction. He was very anxious and shared the gospel with them in his letters, but his mother did not respond. The only thing he could do was to pray for them. He prayed that the Lord would soften his mother's and grandmother's hardened hearts and save them from the grip of false gods and the bondage of the evil one. During every lunar new year, after all his family members had gone to bed, he would sit at his desk with his table-lamp on, praying all night in tears for their salvation. He had been a Christian for thirteen years and had been praying for their salvation throughout that time. But he had not seen any progress. His mother continued to pray to Buddha, burn joss-sticks and play mah-jong. She was still prejudiced against Christianity and still could not understand the choice he had made. Yuan prayed to God, 'O Lord, You have promised us that, as we believe in You, our family members and we will be saved. I believe in Your promise. But after such a long wait my faith has grown weak. I believe, but my faith is too small. Forgive me, man of little faith, and in Your mercy save my family.'

Notes

1. Steamed bread of corn meal, sorghum meat, etc. in the shape of a circular cone, with a hollow at the bottom (also called *wotou*).
2. Which is a pun of 'gospel'.

Chapter 8

Return to Beijing

The way God calls each person is unique and each person's experience of His grace is different, but we all are heading towards the same destiny. All of His ways are full of wonder and grace. God answered Yuan's prayer for the salvation of his family through sickness.

In May 1945, Yuan received a telegram from his grandmother, telling him that his mother was very ill with a disease that caused her abdomen to fill with water and was bedridden. She said she was too old and his sister too young to take care of the family, and she hoped that he could come home as soon as possible to take care of his mother. Yuan was very concerned when he received the letter. His mother had always been opposed to his work in the villages and, since the death of his father, she had written many letters, with all sorts of pretexts, to urge him to return to Beijing. Was this another one of her tricks, he wondered? In order to check out the real situation, he did not reply immediately but wrote to Mr Wang MingDao, saying, 'I have received a letter from my grandmother telling me that my mother is very ill and is bedridden. I wonder whether this is true, or whether it is a trick to make me return to Beijing? I don't know what I should do. Would you be so kind as to send someone round to the house to check out the situation and let me know so that I can make a wise decision?' No sooner had Mr Wang read the letter than he sent his co-worker to the family home. When he saw Yuan's mother lying on the bed, with her whole body swollen, he could see straightaway that she very sick. Mr Wang immediately wrote a letter back to Yuan, saying, 'Your mother is really very ill. No one is taking care of the house.' After he had read the letter, Yuan left his ministry in the village and returned to Beijing with his wife and three children, arriving back in June 1945. This was only his second trip to Beijing since he had followed Rev. Pattee to Hebei in the summer of 1940.

At that time Yuan's mother and grandmother lived at a rented house in Zhushi Street in Beijing. His late father had rented the house, subletting some of the rooms as a source of income. But since his death, his mother and grandmother could no longer take care of such a big house and only rented two of the rooms. When Yuan came home with his family, they occupied one room, while his mother and grandmother shared one of the rooms that had formerly been rented out.

When Yuan first saw his mother lying on the bed, he was very shocked. Not only was her stomach badly swollen but her face, which used to be quite skinny, was also so badly swollen that it was even difficult for her to smile, and it had turned a yellowish colour. She could hardly even move her eyes. She was losing her hair and was almost bald. Yuan had to fight back the tears. He comforted her and told her not to be afraid. She shook her head helplessly, saying that she would not live long.

Yuan was overcome with grief and guilt at having not taken good care of his mother. In the village his income was very limited. His mother and grandmother in Beijing had been living on their savings, which were about to run out. Now he could not afford a better doctor for his mother. For himself, Yuan was very insistent about not taking medication and only relying on the healing power of the Lord. He began to plead with God for the healing and salvation of his mother.

There was an Assembly of God church near the house in Zhushi Street and Yuan would go there to pray for his mother. The pastor of the church approached him and talked to him. When he discovered that Yuan was also a pastor and had served the Lord in the villages for many years, he invited

Yuan to write some articles for their monthly magazine, *Victorious Christian Living*, and asked him to preach at the church on Sunday. Yuan accepted his invitation. He began to get to know the co-workers at the AOG, and a woman by the name of Hannah Wong began to visit the home regularly and to pray with HuiZhen for his mother. He also came into contact with a Christian doctor by the name of Mr Yu who worked at Tongren Hospital. When Mr Yu realised the circumstances, he offered to provide free medical care for his mother. The believers who visited her shared the gospel with her, but she still did not respond. Yuan prayed even harder for her, asking God to soften her hardened heart and save her.

One evening, as Yuan's mother lay in bed, she suddenly saw a man in a white robe standing in front of her bed. He handed her a packet of yellow powder, and she ate it. After a while, Yuan's grandmother came to her and said, 'It's time to take your medicine.' She said, 'Haven't I just taken it?' Her mother was puzzled and asked, 'Who gave you the medicine?' She said, 'A man in a white robe. I didn't know him.' Her mother asked, 'What medicine did you take?' She replied, 'It was a packet of yellow powder. I really have taken the medicine.' No sooner had she finished speaking than she fell asleep. Yuan's grandmother was bewildered. She went and told Yuan what had happened and he was also very puzzled. 'No one gave any medicine to Mum, and there is no stranger in this house. Could she possibly have seen a vision? Perhaps God revealed Himself to her in this way so that she would experience His healing power,' he thought. He said to his grandmother, 'If she doesn't want to take the medicine, let it be.' He immediately went to his room and prayed, 'O God, I give thanks for all that You've done for us. If what happened just now was Your miracle, reveal it to us, so that we can testify to Your greatness.'

From the next day onwards, his mother's swelling began to go down. When Dr Yu came for her regular check up, he measured her stomach and told Yuan that her condition had improved. Yuan shouted to the Lord in praise and told Dr Yu about the incident the night before. They praised the Lord together. From that day onwards, she no longer needed medication and her condition steadily improved each day. Finally, the swelling disappeared completely and her hair began to grow again. She also regained the sparkle in her eyes and her appetite. It was not long before she was up and about again.

Having had a narrow escape from death, Yuan's mother became a new person. She had experienced God's mighty power and would say to everyone she met, 'Thank God. He has healed my disease. I did not believe in Him, but He healed me with His own hands so that I would see His mighty power. Now I'm a believer, and I'm no longer burning joss-sticks or chanting to Buddha or worshipping those false gods.' As a staunch Buddhist she had been used to experiencing trances and, when she was in a trance, she could hold a burning coal with her hand without getting burnt. After she believed in the Lord she changed completely. Yuan's grandmother was approaching seventy then. She had been worshipping Buddha all her life, but when she witnessed what God had done in her daughter's life she joined her in destroying the idols, and turned from worshipping idols to the living God.

Yuan could not help but thank God in tears. He had been praying for the salvation of his family for thirteen years, pleading with God to break down the dividing wall between them because of his faith, so that they could truly be a united family in the Lord. He had asked God to heal and bind up all the wounds in his family. Their relationships had been strained by much hurt, and God's love was the only remedy. Finally, that day had come. He looked back on how his family members had persecuted him when he was a new convert. At that time, he had not been able to understand why God had allowed this to happen to him and had asked God more than once, 'Why do You give me parents who don't understand me? Why does persecution always come from my family? Why does my relationship with my family not improve but has grown worse since I believed in You?' Now he understood that all this had happened according to the perfect will of God. The persecution from his family was allowed by God to mould him and God had turned it into a blessing in disguise, for him as well as his family.

From June 1945 to the winter of that year, Yuan and his family (seven altogether) lived on his weekly preaching and part-time translation job. Although life was hard, they were very joyful. After thirteen years of knowing Jesus, it was the first time they were able to worship God as an entire family. How difficult and precious this was to him. His mother's health was improving steadily. Now Yuan had a new plan. When his mother's health was stable, he would return to his ministry in the village, taking his mother and grandmother with him.

One day, after he had been praying at the AOG church, a Dane by the name of John came to look for Yuan. John's father was an AOG missionary who had come to spread the gospel in China. John had been born in China and could therefore speak the Beijing dialect fluently. When the Japanese surrendered after eight years of occupation, civil war between the Communists and the Nationalists had erupted, and the Americans had set up a committee to mediate the conflict between the two parties. Its head-quarters were located at Xiehe Hospital in Beijing. Due to his bilingual ability, John served on the committee as an interpreter. Now that the Japanese had surrendered, there was a great demand for English speakers, but they were few and far between – the new generation of Chinese spoke Japanese. John had heard Yuan preach a few times and had been favourably impressed by him. He was also aware that Yuan had a good command of English and was struggling to make ends meet, so he offered him work as an interpreter with the committee. At that time, the committee was badly in need of an interpreter and the salary was quite high. But Yuan told him, 'I'm a minister of the gospel and that is my only occupation. I will not consider a full-time secular job.'

On hearing this, John admired Yuan's faithfulness to the Lord. He asked Yuan, 'Are you willing to work part time to make ends meet, so long as it doesn't interfere with your ministry?' Yuan said that he would consider it. John told him about an American-turned-Chinese school in Dongsi. The school had been taken over by the Japanese but, following Japanese surrender, it should have been returned to the Americans. As they were not in a position to do anything for the time being, John had taken it over and had transformed it into a restaurant and hotel for foreigners. Many Americans being released from the concentration camp in Wei District, Shandong, had to come to Beijing to shop and arrange their flight back to the USA, and most of them stayed at the hotel, so business was quite good. Since John was working on the mediating committee, he had no time to take care of the business in the hotel, and was looking for someone to help him. After some consideration, Yuan agreed to take on the job, but insisted he could only work half days because he needed to spread the gospel in the afternoon, and sometimes he needed to preach and lead meetings. John was delighted at the prospect of having his help and agreed to let him work half days. Yuan worked as a cashier and registrar at the hotel-cum-restaurant. When he was free he could spend time praying and sometimes he even had time to write some articles for Christian publications.

One day in the autumn of 1945, Yuan was reading a Christian article at the counter when a Norwegian pastor came to check into the hotel. This Norwegian AOG pastor, Arnult Solvoll, had a Chinese name – Su ChaoSheng. Pastor Su worked in the area of Xinbaoan in Hebei and had come to Beijing for dental treatment. Yuan arranged a room for him and had the porter take him to the room. For the next few days, when Pastor Su went out for his dental treatment, he would greet Yuan but they did not talk much. After about a week, Pastor Su came down to talk to Yuan and asked him in Mandarin, 'Are you a Christian?' Yuan answered in the affirmative and asked, 'How do you know?' Pastor Su said, 'I saw an English Bible on your desk and some Christian literature. I have also seen you reading the Bible sometimes.' This was how they became friends.

One day, Pastor Su invited Yuan to his room and asked him, 'Can you read music?' When Yuan told him he could, Pastor Su said that he had heard someone singing some songs from the hymnbook *Jesus' Family*. He liked the songs but could not read the simplified music scores in which they were written, so he could not learn the songs by himself. He asked Yuan, 'Can you do me a favour and translate all this simplified notation into regular notation?' Yuan said, 'No problem. Give me the hymnbook and I will translate whenever I'm free.' The first song Yuan translated for Pastor Su was Psalm 23, 'The Lord is my Shepherd'.

From then on Yuan's relationship with Pastor Su grew and they talked about each other's beliefs and ministry. When Pastor Su learnt that Yuan had worked in the village in Hebei for five years, their similar ministry experience drew them closer. They talked about their gains and losses and their feelings about their ministry, and shared their vision for their present and future ministry. One afternoon, when Pastor Su was sharing with Yuan about his intention to start a ministry in Beijing, he asked his friend if he was interested. Yuan said, 'There are already many pastors working in Beijing. They don't need us. I came back here because my mother was sick. I'm going back to the village. Eighty per cent of China's population live in villages. But there are too few churches and pastors there. That's where I'm called to serve. Though the life is difficult, working for God is sweet. When my mother's health is stable, I'll take my whole family back to the village.'

In 1946 the negotiations between the Communists and the Nationalists broke down and the situation in China worsened. In order to implement their strategy of surrounding cities with villages, the Communists destroyed the railway in Hebei. The area around the cities became constricted, and it became more difficult for Yuan to achieve his aim of getting back to the village. By then Yuan's grandmother was approaching eighty. More than once she had said that she would not follow him to the countryside. If Yuan insisted on going, she would stay in Beijing alone. This left Yuan in a dilemma. His grandmother had only one daughter (his mother). Apart from Yuan's family, she had no other relatives, and he could not leave her in the city alone without anyone to care for her.

During this period, Yuan felt very much at a loss. He very much wanted to return to the countryside, but circumstances mitigated against it. In the beginning, it had been his mother's ill health, followed by the chaos of the civil war; now, his wife was pregnant with their fourth child and she could not travel long distances. He kept having to delay his return, and he did not know how much longer this would go on. He prayed earnestly for God to guide him about the direction of his future ministry. He did not know why God was not allowing him to return to the countryside. He humbly searched his soul, fearing that the Lord might have abandoned him because of his sins. Although he did not realise it at the time, God was training him to understand His will. He told himself that although some things might be in accordance with God's will, they might not be in accordance with His timing. So he had to be patient. Sometimes he felt very down. He did not know that God was going to give him a new task through this waiting period. God was reminding him that, as His servant, it does not so much matter where you serve Him as whether you are in accordance with His will and serve Him wholeheartedly. He did not know how God would guide his future, but he knew that he should waste no more time and get back to his ministry as soon as possible, so that he could be wholly used by God.

One afternoon, Pastor Su and he were translating the hymnbook in the hotel room. Towards evening Pastor Su said, 'Let's take a rest and go for a walk. We need some fresh air.' They went for a bicycle ride through the streets, roaming aimlessly and chatting. As they approached the city gates, Pastor Su noticed a chapel by the roadside. The signboard above the door was still there, but the chapel was closed and sealed. Yuan was curious. The two men got off their bicycles to take a closer look. It was clear from the date and the red emblem printed on the seal that it had been imposed by the Nationalist government. When they looked through the window, they could see that the interior had an area of more than ten square metres and could accommodate a congregation of about two to three hundred. There were pews, an organ and a pulpit. In fact, it was rather a nice chapel. They were very puzzled about why the church should remain empty, and made some enquiries. The shopkeeper in the shop next to the church told them that the church caretaker lived in a small house behind the chapel. They found the man and he told them that the church had been rented by a Japanese pastor by the name of Oda Kaneo. After the Japanese surrender, he had been sent to the concentration camp in Dongdan, and was there awaiting repatriation. The Nationalist government, having not investigated the matter thoroughly, thought the building was a Japanese asset when in reality it had been rented, not bought. It still belonged to a Chinese by the name of Li ShaoPeng, who had been forced to lose his rent from the chapel.

The Japanese pastor, Oda Kaneo, who had studied in the USA, was a well-known missionary to China and had led the Chinese Christian Fellowship. Yuan had heard of him but had not had any contact with him. Pastor Su and Yuan asked the caretaker for the landlord's address as they were interested in renting the chapel. He told them, 'The landlord is Li ShaoPeng. He lives in No. 19 Bingbuwan. I'm sure he wants to rent it out.' They had another look at the building before they left and discovered that it was actually quite large, equivalent in size to three shops. In the whole compound altogether there were twelve rooms and a courtyard. It was an ideal place to hold meetings. They were very happy to have discovered it and fixed an appointment to talk to the landlord.

Yuan shared their idea with his wife. HuiZhen was by nature a cautious woman and she advised him, 'Don't rush into any decisions. Pray first; see if this is God's will. Then there are many factors to consider. If it really is God's will, He will not only provide you with a meeting place He will also open up the way for you and give you peace. Let's wait on God in prayer.' After praying for a few days, Yuan felt peace of mind. During that period he visited the chapel alone, pacing up and down the church compound. He felt more and more convinced that this was a very good place for a meeting. It was situated at the hub of Beijing's transport and commerce systems. Furthermore, it was near the White

Pagoda Temple, which held two feasts every month. People flocked to the temple feasts from all over the city. Some people went for business, while others took their families to the feasts, or went there to meet friends. It was a golden opportunity for evangelism. They could make good use of the church building and could save themselves the trouble and money of renting meeting places.

For Yuan, who had worked in the villages for so many years and had lost touch with urban evangelism in Beijing, this was a good and important opportunity for him to get involved again. He began to like this place more and more. He would often go and look in through the window at the pews, the blackboard and pulpit. They were both familiar and new to him at the same time. They were new, because he had not worked there before, but they were familiar because they were the tools of his trade as a pastor. He felt peace and joy in his heart, replacing the previous anxiety he had felt.

One day he rode his bicycle to the sealed church with his six-year-old son. He picked FuYin up in his arms and let him look in through the window. FuYin asked, 'Dad, what is this?' Yuan replied, 'This is a place to spread the gospel.' FuYin then asked, 'Who owns it?' Yuan said, 'What would you think about us spreading the gospel in this place?' FuYin said, 'Great! I like this place. Let's spread the gospel together.' His son's words made Yuan very happy. He was planning to talk to the landlord, but he was still afraid that it might just be his own idea and not God's. He was afraid that his own desires might get in the way of God's. He prayed, 'O God, if this is Your will, let it come into being and let the landlord agree to rent it out to me without any difficulty and with a reasonable rent. If this is not Your will, please put barriers in the way. Show me Your will so that I will know what to do.'

Before he went to see the landlord, he discussed with Pastor Su whether or not they should go together. They decided it was better for Yuan to go alone, as, after his previous bad experience of having the building sealed as a result of it being rented out to a foreigner, the landlord might be reluctant to do the same thing again. So Yuan rode his bicycle to No. 19 Bingbuwan to look for the landlord. He managed to find him without much difficulty. The landlord, Li ShaoPeng, was an outspoken middle-aged man who was very happy to hear that Yuan wanted to rent his building. He poured out his grievances to Yuan, complaining about how unfairly he had been treated by the Nationalist government when they had sealed his building. For the last six months, he had travelled backwards and forwards to the city council, pleading his case but to no avail. Not only was he losing rent but he was also wasting a lot of time and money talking to various officers, who refused to settle the issue.

Finally he said to Yuan dejectedly, 'I'm willing to rent the chapel out to you, but before you can do so the city council will have to approve the unsealing of the building. Otherwise, I can do nothing – even if you were to pay me 5 kg of gold every day. I don't think there's much hope of the seal being opened at the moment. Common people like you and me seldom have the chance to talk to the officials, let alone to ask them a favour. Why don't we discuss the rent first and then, if you feel that the amount is reasonable and still want to proceed, we can try to negotiate with the city council to open the seal? If you can't accept the rent, then we can save ourselves all the trouble.'

The landlord was tired of liaising with the government and he was making it plain that, if Yuan wanted to rent the building, he was going to have to liaise with the government on his own. Yuan liked his frankness and thought what he was saying was reasonable. After a few rounds of discussions, they agreed on a monthly rent of the price of 150 kg of millet. During the civil war, the value of the currency was constantly fluctuating and, due to serious devaluation, it could no longer serve as an accurate measure for prices. They would still trade in banknotes, but the amount of the payment in money differed according to the fluctuating price of 150 kg of millet. It was an indication of the uncertain socio-economic situation.

Having agreed the rent, the next step was to liaise with the city council to open the seal. Yuan did not have any relatives in Beijing, and he had not been born there. Having spent the last few years in the village and around churches, he did not have any contacts in the governmental departments. Above all, he knew that he was not good at this. Actually, apart from spreading the gospel, there was almost nothing else he was good at. As a foreigner, Pastor Su was not much help either. After spending some time talking about it, they felt a bit despondent, but they immediately felt rebuked for their attitude. Yuan was angry with himself: 'Why have I forgotten to come to the Lord in prayer? This is God's work. If this is in accordance with His will, He will open a way for us. Things that are impossible in man's sight are not impossible in God's sight. Why am I a man of such little faith? How can I be put down by such an insignificant difficulty and forget that God is my resource? How wretched I am!' So, Yuan prayed in his room and cast his worry on God. What happened in these negotiations would serve as an indication of God's approval, or otherwise, of his ministry in the chapel in Beijing. He arranged a date to go to the city council office. Pastor Su and he decided not to give any gift or bribe to the officials but to leave the outcome to God.

After Japanese surrender, the US troops were selling their redundant goods for civilian use at very low prices. A Jeep cost only US $500, which was extremely cheap. When he heard about this, Pastor Su went to Tianjin to buy one. Although very cheap, the Jeep he purchased was still in good condition and he felt it was worth the money. Yuan and Pastor Su modified the Jeep and painted it white with the words 'gospel vehicle' on both sides and the rear. Whenever Pastor Su drove it, he attracted a large crowd and he would give out gospel tracts.

On the day Yuan and Pastor Su went to the city council, they went in the Jeep. When they arrived at the sentry, the official was very polite to them. They made their way to the office dealing with the sealing of Japanese properties. The officials there, assuming that Pastor Su was an American, treated him like a special guest, as Americans were held in high regard in China at that time. On hearing the case, the official promised to get the matter resolved as soon as possible. After that, he gave Pastor Su his name card and said, 'You are always welcome to see me if you are in trouble.

I'll do my best to help you.' The officer even escorted them
to the gate and shook their hands. They never imagined that
the problem would be solved so easily. As they walked out
of the city council office, they were so happy that they
couldn't help but laugh. This was indeed the grace of God,
opening a way for them.

When Yuan looked closely at the official's name card, he
had another surprise. This official, by the name of Mr Liu,
lived in the same building as Mr Wang KeChen, Yuan's
teacher. Wang KeChen was Wang MingDao's partner. He
had taught Yuan mathematics at the YMCA school and they
still kept in touch after all these years and were quite close.
When Yuan told Pastor Su about this, they decided to call in
at Mr Wang KeChen's house and talk to him.

That afternoon, Yuan took Pastor Su to see Mr Wang
KeChen. He approved of their plan to begin a church in
Beijing, and was glad that they had found such an ideal
venue. He told them that Mr Liu lived in the same building
and that both families got along very well. He thought that
the church must have been sealed by mistake and there
should not be any problem opening it up. He advised Yuan to
continue to pray and wait quietly on the Lord. He would talk
to his neighbour and, if it was God's will, their plan to open a
church would be realised.

In the days that followed, Yuan prayed on the one hand,
and prepared for the opening of the new church on the
other. At that time he was still working as a cashier at John's
hotel-cum-restaurant part time, and spending the afternoons
sharing the gospel or translating Christian literature. In his
leisure time, he would imagine his ministry in the new
church. His faith had grown stronger and stronger and he
could not wait to start. Two weeks later, the city council sent
some officers to inform Li ShaoPeng that they had mis-
takenly sealed his property, believing it to belong to the
Japanese. They had decided to open the seal and return
the property to him. He immediately informed Yuan, adding
that he had never imagined that the problem would be
resolved so soon. He gave him the keys and reminded him
of the rent they had agreed. Yuan went to find Pastor Su and

together they went to the church. The seal had already been broken and so they were able to enter the building for the first time. There was a thick layer of dust covering everything and, though some of the furniture was not in good order, it was well furnished.

Yuan was excited to discover a small cellar in front of the podium, covered by a wooden lid. When he opened the lid, he saw it was a baptismal pool. He was delighted. As it had not been visible through the window his first plan on taking possession of the building had been to make a baptismal pool. God had provided everything for him. That would save a considerable amount of money. He said to his wife, 'God really does have mercy on us. He knows that we can't afford much, so He has provided us with a well-furnished church that does not need any renovation. Now all we have to do is to clean the place and put up some banners.' HuiZhen said, 'I'll take care of that. I'll do the cleaning, as well as the writing of the banners.'

The next day, with her eldest son, FuYin, HuiZhen took some brooms and other tools to clean the church. The task was accomplished within two days. FuYin, who had already grown up into a mature boy, helped his mother with the cleaning. There was some heavier work involving some climbing which Yuan needed to do after his work at the hotel. After working hard for a few days, the place was spotless. HuiZhen bought some brushes and ink, and wrote verses on banners, to be put up on both sides of the window. The verses were, *'There is a way that seems right to a man but in the end it leads to death'* (Proverbs 14:12) and *'For the wages of sin is death but the gift of God is eternal life'* (Romans 6:23). She was very skilful and the calligraphy was beautiful. She also decorated the panes of glass in the windows with some simple pictures with evangelistic messages. They turned the old, dusty building into a bright shining church. Yuan's whole family prepared to move into the building and begin his new ministry within the next few days.

One afternoon, Pastor Su dropped by. He was delighted when he saw the refurbished building. To Yuan's surprise he took out a measurement tape to measure the signboard above

the door. He asked him curiously, 'What are you doing?'
Pastor Su replied, 'I'm measuring the signboard. How can you
make a new one if you don't know the measurements?' Yuan
was perplexed. He asked, 'Why can't we use the old one?
Why waste money on a new one if we still can use the old
one?' Pastor Su said, 'Look at what it says. Can we use that?'
Although old, the inscription was still clear, especially since
Yuan had just dusted it a few days ago. It said 'Gospel Hall'.
Yuan didn't have a clue about why they couldn't use it.
Pastor Su said, 'We belong to the AOG; we should have the
name of the AOG up there, not Gospel Hall.'

Yuan was stunned. Up until now Pastor Su had been saying
to him that they were co-workers. He had not thought about
their denominational differences. Now it seemed that these
differences were beginning to pose a problem. Yuan said to
Pastor Su, 'I'm not going to change the board. We'll use this
one.' Pastor Su said, 'No way! If we don't use the AOG's
name, the AOG association will not support us and you'd
have a problem with the rent, your salary, and the general
expenses of the church. This is a new church. So don't expect
to be able to manage with just the collection of offerings. It'll
be difficult to even make ends meet, let alone expand the
work.'

Now Yuan understood Pastor Su's intention. He hoped that
the AOG association would run the church and cover the
expenses. But Yuan would not accept this. While believing
that Christian workers should co-operate, he was convinced
that they should depend solely on the Lord for their livelihood. Otherwise, they would be putting their trust in
organisations and men instead of God. Pastor Su had sound
rationale for his concerns. It was unlikely that, initially, the
collections would meet the needs. It would be much easier if
the church were run by an organisation. But Yuan was very
reluctant to go down this path. He felt that if he joined an
organisation, he would be bound by financial attachments to
the leadership of men. This would deprive them of learning
how to rely on God alone in times of difficulty.

In 1938, after he had completed his theological education,
he could have stayed on at FETS as a lecturer and had a stable

source of income, but he was not willing to be limited by the commitments a regular salary would entail. So he went to Tianjin alone. Even though at that time he was not completely free from church institutions, he had a more independent form of ministry. In 1939, after he had returned to Beijing, he worked as a part-time translator while serving as a pastor and began to experience the freedom of serving the Lord without being bound by the commitments associated with a regular salary. Through such an experience, he was convinced that this was the right way for a Christian pastor to live. He should be directly sent and supported by God. During his five years ministering in the countryside, Yuan was fed by the Lord through his neighbours. His experience during these five years had formed his philosophy and methodology of ministry, and enabled him to implement his own theory of ministry. All these factors combined to strengthen his conviction that a pastor should be directly supported by God in all circumstances, and should not join any organisation or receive a monthly salary, as the unbelievers did.

But many a time a minister of the Lord would face some very real problems. At such times, some solutions seemed more practical than waiting before the Lord in prayer. Christian faith would always be challenged and tested. The problem Yuan was facing right now was a familiar one, but he was very firm in his belief that this was how God had guided him. He expressed his opinion to Pastor Su ChaoSheng, 'I'm genuinely thankful for your thoughtful suggestion. But I'm not willing to join any organisation, especially those run by foreigners. Besides, I don't want to receive a regular salary from any organisation, as the unbelievers do. I'll do whatever work the Lord entrusts to me in this Gospel Hall. If the Lord gives me only one sheep, I'll shepherd one; if two I'll shepherd two. Since I'm a minister of the gospel, I should live on the gospel. If the collection of offerings isn't enough to make ends meet, I will get a part-time job. If I have enough from the collection, I will wholeheartedly do whatever God entrusts to me. I don't care about fame or appearances. I only care about whether I've been faithful to the Lord. I'll give my best for whatever the Lord entrusts to me. God's grace is sufficient for me.'

On hearing this, Pastor Su remained silent for quite a while. Then, he said to Yuan firmly, 'Brother Yuan, you'd better think again. How could you afford the rent for such a huge building? If you refuse to run the church under the auspices of the AOG association, you won't even have a regular income. How are you going to survive? You'd better think about this carefully; don't make a hasty decision. Otherwise, you might regret it in the future. This is for your benefit.' Yuan said, 'I don't need to think about it any more. I thought about this when I was in seminary. I've made up my mind not to join any organisation or receive any regular salary. I don't believe that God will allow me to starve. He will take full responsibility for me. I hope you will respect my position and set aside organisation and money. Let's serve God together in this place and pastor this church, so that we will accomplish whatever God has entrusted to us.' Pastor Su said, 'I'm a Norwegian AOG missionary. I will not leave my denomination. Are there any pastors today who do not receive a regular salary? This is also a means of God's provision. If a Church backs you up, it's beneficial to the expansion of your ministry. At least you don't have to worry about raising support. You'd better not make a hasty decision. Running the church under the AOG association will be a great help. Please reconsider.' Yuan said, 'I believe that the Lord guides every individual differently. In the apostolic era the workers did not receive regular salaries, but their zeal and effectiveness in evangelism was incomparable. If we want to evangelise as effectively as the apostles did, we should imitate their methods. We are all preaching the same Jesus. So don't divide our faith up into various denominations and don't set boundaries according to denominations. I disagree with the suggestion of running the church under the AOG association. I won't join any denomination, nor will I receive payment from any organisation.'

The heated argument continued, with Pastor Su patiently advising Yuan to consider joining the AOG and Yuan insisting that he would not do so. Finally, Pastor Su said, 'In this case, I don't think we can work together. I'll pull out. If you encounter any problems, my door will always be open for you.' He did not believe that Yuan could survive without the support of an organisation. The monthly rent of the price of 150 kg of millet was not a small amount for Yuan. With that, Pastor Su left.

In March 1946, a few days after the city council had broken the seal, the Gospel Hall was officially launched. It was not long before Yuan hit a financial crisis. Before the launching ceremony, he had thought that a number of the old members of the Gospel Hall would return, but to his great disappointment that did not happen, the main reason being that when Oda Kaneo had been the pastor, there had not been many Chinese Christians in his congregation. Besides, he was not very well known in the area and not many Christians knew that he had started a new church. In the first month, Yuan tried to make up the financial deficit by working as a part-time translator at night in addition to his part-time job in John's hotel-cum-restaurant in the afternoon. Sometimes, he worked until midnight. Nevertheless, after working for one month, all his income could not cover the rent and family expenses.

On the date the rent was due, HuiZhen took out her dowry and made up the payment. They had expected it to be difficult, but not quite this difficult. Pastor Su's analysis proved accurate. The financial pressure was immense. But he never imagined that Yuan would not turn to him when faced with such a crisis. Yuan said to his wife, 'No matter what happens, we must wait for the Lord. It doesn't matter if life is hard. This is how God shapes us, to see if we will persevere to the end.'

For Yuan the greatest difficulty was not financial; it was the lack of fruit in his evangelism. During the launching ceremony, Yuan preached to his wife, mother and children seated in the pews. He led the singing of hymns, played the drum and preached. Even though it was quite cold in Beijing at the time, they left all the windows and doors open, hoping that the drumbeats and singing would attract people. Passers-by heard the drumbeats and singing, but they only stood at the door. Yuan repeatedly invited them to come in, but they refused. The more he invited them, the more reticent they became until finally they left. A few of them came in and asked, 'What's going on here? Are you selling medicine?' They did not know what 'Gospel Hall' meant. They thought the word 'hall' meant a pharmacy. When they discovered it was a religious meeting place, they left. On that day, Yuan preached to his family members on the topic, 'How to come to the Lord in prayer'. His sermon was very brief. Afterwards, the whole family prayed together for the ministry of the Gospel Hall.

Yuan learnt a lesson from the failure of this first service, which he implemented for the second. Instead of singing and playing the drum inside the building he changed his tactic and took the music outside the church. Early in the morning he had all his family members stand in a row and together they sang a simple chorus over and over again: 'All have sinned, all have sinned. Jesus Christ was crucified on the cross to save sinners.' This tactic really worked and people began to gather round! They continued singing until a crowd had formed, and then he began to preach, saying, 'We're sharing the gospel with you. If you want eternal life, listen! This gospel is given to us as a free gift; you don't need to pay a single cent for it. Those who receive it will possess eternal life and can go to heaven.' When the people heard that they did not have to pay a single cent, they were attracted and some of them came into the church. So, Yuan returned to the pulpit and began to preach the gospel. A few of them lost their patience and left halfway through the sermon. Others stayed to the end, but did not respond. They never appeared again.

Evangelism is not a simple task. It demands great patience and persistence, and it also requires methods and techniques. While praying earnestly for his work of evangelism, Yuan said to himself, 'Be patient. I'm only a sower. God is the One who enables the seeds to grow. I should work without asking for results – the field is not ripe for harvest yet.' He continued with the work, holding on to a sincere hope. Three times a week he and his whole family lined up outside the church to sing hymns and play the drum, preaching the gospel in a simple way. When there was a special feast at the temple, he would use this golden opportunity for an extra gospel rally.

Shortly after the launch of the Gospel Hall, Yuan went to visit Oda Kaneo in the Dongdan Concentration Camp. Since most of the items in the church had originally belonged to the Japanese missionary before being confiscated by the government and given to the landlord, Yuan felt that he should go and introduce himself, and thank him personally before he was repatriated.

When he arrived at the concentration camp, he told the guard whom he was looking for. The guard asked him who Oda Kaneo was, and Yuan told him that he was a friend. The guard went inside for a moment before returning. He took Yuan to a house where, shortly afterwards, Oda Kaneo was brought to him. Yuan told him, 'I've rented out the Gospel Hall. It had been sealed by the government and I've managed to have the seal opened by the city council. Right now I'm running a church on the premises. I'm using the pews, pulpit and other furniture you left. I wanted to let you know and to express my sincere gratitude.' Quite unexpectedly, Oda Kaneo was very angry. He said in Chinese, 'I don't mind you using my furniture. After all, there's not much of value anyway. But how can you use my church building without my consent?' Yuan explained, 'Firstly, I did not break the seal. The Nationalist Government opened it, and the landlord gave me the keys. Secondly, although you used to rent the place, when you were sent to this concentration camp the building was sealed and then returned to the landlord. Whatever agreement you had with the landlord, in the situation he had full authority to deal with his property as he saw fit.' Oda Kaneo was still very unhappy about it. He insisted that Yuan should have consulted him and asked for his permission before he used the premises. Yuan did not hold any grudge against him and tried to understand where he was coming from. Perhaps it was the strain of being in the concentration camp that had caused him to react like this. Since he had had the best of intentions, he did not take the fact that his efforts were not appreciated to heart. After all, the church was rented legally.

During the first month, even though the services were mainly attended by Yuan's own family members, he did not take the singing and preaching lightly. He knew that, in the absence of obvious results, he needed to be on his toes all the more. His whole family often gathered and prayed earnestly for Yuan's ministry, particularly for a suitable co-worker.

One afternoon, when Yuan was sitting reading in one of the pews, he heard someone knocking at the door. The door was not closed, and Yuan invited the person to come in. A very kind-looking bearded old man with a broad forehead and sparkling eyes was standing at the door. Touching his beard he smiled and looked inside. Yuan put down his book and went to invite the old man to come in. The visitor asked, 'Who is the pastor of this church?' Yuan said, 'I am. My surname is Yuan. Don't address me as Rev. Yuan. Call me Pastor or Mr Yuan.' The old man said, 'I'm also a Christian. I was passing and was very happy, so I stood at the door to have a look.' Yuan could tell from his accent that he came from Beijing. He asked, 'What's your name? Judging from your accent, you're from Beijing, aren't you?' The old man said, 'My name is Xia LuChuan, from Beijing. I've been a Christian for many years. I'm so glad to see the growing number of people who are giving their lives to serve the Lord.' They talked to each other and enjoyed their conversation very much. As a native of Beijing, Mr Xia gave Yuan a lot of useful suggestions about his ministry in the city, which Yuan jotted down. After a long conversation, Mr Xia left. Yuan invited Mr Xia to stay for dinner, but he refused. He said that he would come to help at the next meeting. He was true to his word. He shared the gospel with others, ushered them to their seats and helped in all sorts of ways. From that time on, he was the first to arrive and the last to leave at every meeting. He was Yuan's first co-worker. Later, due to the increasing workload, Yuan invited Mr and Mrs Xia to live with them at the church. He said to Mr Xia, 'God has prepared enough space for us, let's enjoy the blessing of living together.'

The Gospel Hall's first convert was Mr Liang DeFang. He came from Wuan District in Hebei, having escaped to Beijing with his wife and daughter from their war-torn home. Sometimes, he worked as a moneychanger in Nanshun Street and was one of the onlookers who watched while Yuan played his drum. Once or twice he also came in and heard Yuan preach. He agreed with what Yuan said about human sinfulness, but his mature age and personality prevented him from responding to the gospel immediately. For a month he just observed and listened.

One day, after Yuan had preached, he did not leave. Yuan went up to him and, after some general conversation, asked him frankly, 'Do you know that we are all sinners?' Most people who were asked this question did not fully understand it. They would simply give a noncommittal answer while feeling that the pastor was being too personal. But Liang DeFang was very different. He replied sincerely, 'You're right. By nature we're evil, not good. I know that I've committed many sins. Although they are not crimes, my conscience reminds me of them.' On hearing this, Yuan thanked God in his heart. Anyone who acknowledges his or her sin is not far from salvation. He asked, 'Since you've admitted your sins, are you willing to receive Jesus as your personal Saviour, so that He can take away all your sins?' Liang DeFang said with firm conviction, 'I'm willing. I'm willing now. I've been searching for so long. Now I've found what I've been looking for.'

After that, Yuan led Liang DeFang in saying the sinner's prayer, with DeFang repeating each sentence after him. After saying the prayer, he said to Yuan, 'I want to say another prayer, will you say it with me?' Yuan answered that he would. After a long silence, DeFang prayed in his tired voice; though stammering, it was the sincere outpouring of his heart. His deep awareness of his own sins and his sincere acceptance of the salvation of Jesus was a confirmation for Yuan that this man belonged to the Lord. He knew that people who had a deep conviction of their own sins, as De Fang had, would have an equally deep experience of God's grace and would grow all the faster in their spiritual life.

Before he left, DeFang said to Yuan, 'Next time I'll bring my wife and daughter, so that they too will receive this blessing.' From that time onwards, whenever Yuan had a meeting, DeFang, his wife and his daughter would sit on the first row. Shortly afterwards, they also accepted Jesus as their Saviour. The conversion of this family was a great encouragement to Yuan. Whenever he introduced DeFang, he would say, 'This is the gift God gave me as a result of my playing the drum.'

Yuan heard that there was a special school for the blind in Balizhuang, Beijing, run by a foreign parachurch organisation. Being a Christian was one of the requirements for admission to the school. Yuan wanted to visit the school, but he kept putting it off because he was afraid that the school might be unhappy about it. One day two blind young men came to the Gospel Hall, and Yuan talked to them after the meeting. They told Yuan that they had come because they had heard that a new church had been started there. Yuan was very touched by their sincerity. He asked them about their school, which turned out to be similar to the YMCA school in that it too was a nominal Christian school with the real agenda being social service. Many blind students claimed that they had accepted Jesus merely to enrol into the school and, therefore, not many of them were born-again Christians. The school did not have a regular Christian meeting and so some of the committed Christians in the school were looking for a church. On hearing this, Yuan asked them, 'It's not so convenient for you to move around. Are there any other ways you can worship together?' Both of them said that they had no idea but they would discuss this with their other friends and would be back. Yuan invited them to stay for lunch and afterwards sent them off to the bus station.

A week later, four or five blind youths, each carrying a cane, came to Yuan's meeting. They were the committed Christians from the special school for the blind. After the meeting, Yuan went straight up to talk to them, not even stopping to have a drink. They told him that they had set out from the school early that morning because they wanted to listen to his preaching. They said that they had learnt a lot and wanted Yuan to lead them in a Bible study. They hoped that Yuan could give them an answer that same day. Yuan decided to have a regular Bible study with them every Tuesday night. He asked, 'It's not very convenient for me to come to your school. Is it possible to find a meeting place?' One of them by the name of Wang DeMing said, 'We don't want to trouble you. I think we'll come here so that you won't have to waste your time travelling.' Yuan appreciated his thoughtfulness, but insisted, 'If we can meet at the school, I'll come there. If you have time and feel comfortable about coming to worship here on Sundays, you're always welcome. That way we can meet twice a week.'

From then on Yuan went to the special school for the blind every Tuesday night. Balizhuang was a long way from the Gospel Hall and Yuan went there by bicycle. During the spring, he often got caught in unpredictable downpours on the way. Sometimes, when it rained before the meeting, the students thought that Yuan would not come, but he would always arrive. During the winter, the weather in Beijing was very cold with a bitter wind from the north, and sometimes it snowed. But regardless of the weather, he was always punctual. His conscientiousness and willingness to oblige made a good impression on the students.

While he was leading their Bible study, Yuan got to know some people who later became very good co-workers in his ministry. A young man by the name of Chen BangHeng was a very talented singer, with a very broad and bright voice, an excellent memory and good sense of rhythm. He also had an incredible ability to learn new songs. If he heard a song played and sung once or twice, he could repeat it perfectly. Recognising his talent, Yuan asked him if he felt led by the Lord to be a worship leader. Initially, he was shy but, through Yuan's encouragement, his confidence began to develop and he became an outstanding worship leader. He always told others that it was Pastor Yuan who had encouraged him. But Yuan said, 'God has given you your talent. You've got a lot to offer. You must learn to rely more on Him and then He will use you to an even greater extent.'

Every Sunday, Yuan had FuYin go to the bus station outside the city gate to bring the young people from the special school for the blind over to the service. After the service, HuiZhen would treat them to lunch. In the beginning, they declined the invitation because they did not want to trouble Mr and Mrs Yuan by making them serve them. It was especially difficult for them as blind people to eat meals in new surroundings, and it required a lot of effort on the part of the Yuan family to make it possible for them. But Yuan would say to them, 'Let's have lunch and after that you can ask me questions.' During lunchtime, HuiZhen was so busy serving their guests that she could only have her lunch when they had finished theirs. After they had finished eating, they had the opportunity to ask Yuan questions. During these question and answer sessions HuiZhen would help those who had torn clothes by repairing them and she would also wash any dirty clothes (getting them to change into Yuan's clothes while she washed them), so that they could wear clean clothes back to school. Sometimes it suddenly rained when they were about to leave and then Yuan would put them up at the church. They felt very much at home and always looked forward to coming to the church even though it was quite a way from their school.

In the autumn of 1946, God opened another door for Yuan's ministry. At that time Beijing was under the rule of the Nationalist Party (Kuomintang). The central broadcasting station opened two channels for gospel broadcasts on 850 kHz and 770 kHz. Each Sunday a Protestant pastor and a Roman Catholic priest would be invited to broadcast through these channels, each of them preaching for half an hour. Wang MingDao and Yuan were among the speakers invited. When it was his turn to preach, the broadcasting company would send a car to fetch him. After preaching at his own church, he would have fellowship with his members while waiting for the car from the central broadcasting station. Once, he was scheduled to speak on the same day as some Roman Catholic priests from the Dingdu Street Monastery. On the way home, he chatted to them in English and shared his experience of being born again with them. He also talked to them about Martin Luther and the Reformation. He invited them over to his church and, later, he also went to see them in their monastery. After several conversations, Yuan came to the conclusion that there were some genuinely born-again believers in both the Greek Orthodox and Roman Catholic Churches. Though they differed with Protestantism in outward form and rituals, they shared the same core beliefs. All of them believed in the cross and God's salvation. Yuan used to tell young people, 'We ought to look up to the strengths of others. There are three things that make the Roman Catholics superior to us: firstly, the vow of celibacy of the Roman Catholic priests; secondly, the vow of poverty of the Roman Catholic priests; and thirdly, their unquestioned obedience to the Pope. I fail to attain all three of these.'

After going through many difficulties and quietly waiting before the Lord, in 1947 their work began to yield fruit. The number of new converts was increasing. There were now about 100 regular worshippers. The Gospel Hall also ran a Sunday school, which sought to evangelise children. Yuan insisted that all children, including his own, had to attend Sunday school while the adult worship service was on. They also received homework, which they were required to do. In the summer of 1947, he baptised the first batch of new converts. They talked to the candidates beforehand to make sure that they were really sure of their salvation before baptising them. From that time on the church had a baptism every summer. The number of those who were baptised increased from around twenty in 1947, to about forty in 1949, and fifty-two in 1952.

In 1947, Yuan was asked by a Swedish couple, John and Andisen (who worked in the desert of North Xiaxi), to help a young Swedish missionary by the name of Asta Nilson, known by her Chinese name Aixide. After her conversion Aixide had been called by the Lord to be a missionary in China, but because she could not speak Chinese, she was encountering a lot of difficulties. Yuan invited her to attend the meetings at his church. He encouraged her to introduce herself in Chinese and told her, 'There is only one way to learn a language rapidly – talk more with the locals.' Ms Aixide liked to be with HuiZhen, who gently gave her advice on how to live in a foreign country. HuiZhen said to her, 'Make yourself at home. Tell me if you have any problems. We're family. Don't be shy.' When Yuan talked with Ms Aixide about the development of churches in China, he said, 'Chinese Christians should build their own independent and self-supporting churches. I'm earning my living by working as a translator part time, which also helps cover the expenses of the church. Chinese churches should work towards being self-supporting and self-propagating.' From their keen involvement in worship and ministry, Aixide knew that the believers in the Gospel Hall were really children of the Kingdom.

Ms Aixide went on to minister in places like Inner Mongolia and Tianjin but she still kept in touch with the Yuans. When she was working in Tianjin, they often had the opportunity to visit her. Whenever Yuan met her, he would ask her about her progress with the language and would spend time giving her some tuition. At that time, China was in the process of changing government and many missionaries were pulling out of the country. Yuan encouraged her to work hard on improving her Chinese so that she could respond to God's call to become a missionary who preached among the Chinese in China. One of the principles of conduct for a Christian worker that he taught her was, whatever circumstances she was in, to hold on to the Word of God. In 1951, Ms Aixide went to Hong Kong to fulfil her call to be a missionary among the Chinese. She always remembered what Yuan had told her. Her forty-year ministry in Hong Kong was greatly influenced by the help given by the Yuans in those early years.

In the latter part of 1947, Yuan resigned from his secular jobs and concentrated all his energies on his work as a pastor. In 1949, the membership increased to 200. Yuan put up a banner outside the Gospel Hall: 'Turn back! Why should you perish?' which could be seen clearly from quite a distance. It even saved the life of a young man from the north-eastern part of China who was about to commit suicide. The young man had been exiled to Beijing. In utter despair, he was about to commit suicide by jumping into the Fucheng River when, at that crucial moment, he looked up and saw the words over the Gospel Hall: 'Turn back! Why should you perish?' They had a profound impact on him. He thought, 'Isn't this speaking to me? Is suicide my only option?' He paced up and down, hesitating to take this drastic final step. Eventually, he decided to go inside the church, hoping to meet the author of the banner. He went to the door of the Gospel Hall and fortunately Yuan was there. When he saw him, Yuan asked the distraught young man what the matter was. The young man couldn't speak, and tears were streaming down his face. He just sobbed and sobbed, eventually pouring out all of his grief and despair to Yuan. He told him that he had been on the brink of committing suicide when he had seen the banner. Yuan said, 'Young man, you've come to the right place. I may not fully understand how desperate your problems are, but I want to tell you that you have no right to take your own life. For God is your Creator and life is His gift. Believe in Jesus and you'll be able to value your life. Life will become worth living again.' The young man later believed in Jesus and began to attend Yuan's church. Later, he returned to his home town with a joyful heart.

When the Communists came to power, before the liberation of China, the future looked bleak to many pastors and many of them fled abroad. The principal of FETS, Mr Wu Zhi, came to tell Yuan that the Anglican Church was looking for a pastor who could speak English and Cantonese to work in Indonesia. He felt that Yuan was a suitable candidate and wanted to offer him this opportunity. He told Yuan, 'You must pray about this. If it's God's will, then you should go. If not, then don't go.' Yuan said, 'I won't go. God called me to serve Him in China. There are so many lost souls in China. I'll stay here and work wholeheartedly and faithfully on what God has entrusted to me.' In the period from the end of 1948 to 1949, many missionaries were leaving China. A pastor by the surname of Rui who worked in Beijing told Yuan, 'I'm afraid that it will be difficult to spread the gospel now that the Communists have taken over China. It's quite possible that Christians will be persecuted. If you want to leave China, it's not too late. We'll take you with us. You've got a good command of English. I'm sure you won't have a problem surviving in a foreign country.' Yuan said, 'My burden is for China. Why should I go abroad? The Communists are propagating a policy of religious freedom. I don't think they'll go overboard. Besides, I was called to serve God in China, and He will make a way for me. '

On 3 February 1949, the People's Liberation Army (PLA) sent its first batch of troops into Beijing. They marched through the city gate right past Yuan's Gospel Hall. HuiZhen had already sealed the glass in the church windows, to prevent it being shattered when the army marched through the city. She had also hoarded some food, fearing that prices might rise. But Yuan said that she was being overanxious. Seeing that the troops were very well disciplined, he was not very worried. He did not believe that they would create trouble. He took the view that as a Christian pastor he had nothing to do with politics and as long as he stayed away from politics and committing any offence against the State, there should not be any problem continuing his ministry.

The government had changed, the circumstances had changed, but Yuan's determination to spread the gospel never changed.

PART IV

'I know my Redeemer lives'

Chapter 9

Troubles Brought about by the Three-Self Patriotic Movement

On 3 February 1949, the PLA entered Beijing. On 23 February, churches in Beijing formed the Beiping Christian Association to discuss how to respond to the political changes and survive under Communist rule. In the beginning, many pastors succumbed to 'floating anxieties', their greatest concern being whether the atheistic Communist government would create trouble for the Church and, if so, how they should respond.

As always, Yuan took the change calmly. When some believers shared their anxieties with him, he would smile and advise them, 'Don't be overly concerned. Firstly, we are only spreading the gospel and have nothing against the government. It does not really matter who is in power. We will still continue our work. We're working for God, not for any man or government. Secondly, the Communists are not as bad as the rumours make out. The rumour that property and wives are being shared is too ridiculous to be true. One of their principles is freedom of religion. The PLA has entered Beijing, but everything is still OK. They won't create any trouble for us. Don't worry.'

He was not merely comforting others, this was what he sincerely believed. He had quite a high regard for the Communists, and thought that they were highly disciplined, which was in fact true. Throughout 1949, the Communists did not make things difficult for Christians and pastors. But this did not mean that it would always be like that.

In the winter of 1949, Yuan took a few Christians with him to play the drum and preach the gospel on White Pagoda Temple Street. People soon gathered round when they heard the drumbeats and Yuan began to preach the gospel to them. As he was speaking, suddenly a voice shouted, 'Clear the street! Don't gather there!' The whole crowd disbanded in a minute. A few soldiers stood in front of Yuan and his partners. The one in charge asked them, 'What are you doing here? Why are you making so much noise in the street? Who sent you here?' Yuan knew that they were facing members of the PLA. He answered, 'We are preaching the gospel, as we have done in the past.' The head soldier looked Yuan up and down, and seeing that he was a gentle and skinny man, said, 'You're not allowed to have a public gathering here. Follow me to the office of the Army Control Committee.'[1] They confiscated Yuan's drum and the other instruments they had with them and took him and his friends to the office of the Army Control Committee at Xisi. When they arrived at the office, the head soldier was less harsh than before and asked Yuan, 'What is your occupation?' Yuan replied, 'I'm pastor of the Gospel Hall. My name is Yuan.' The man nodded and said, 'Next time, don't preach on the street. Is that clear?' Yuan asked, 'Haven't you Communists promised freedom of religion?' He was implying that, if the Communists had promised freedom of religion, why then were they forbidding him to preach on the street? The man was taken aback and, in an even gentler tone of voice, explained, 'We do indeed promote freedom of religion. But at the moment China has just been liberated, and the situation is a bit chaotic. You'd better meet inside the church. Now you can claim back your belongings which were confiscated.' Yuan was impressed by his friendliness and did not say anything else. After that, they went back to the church. From then on, they no longer preached on the street, but they would leave all the windows and doors open whenever they met so that people outside the church might be attracted. Sometimes, people would stop and look in when they heard the noise.

In the early period after liberation, the political situation was still very unsettled so religious issues were not the government's immediate concern. Their highest priority was social order. So for about a year people still enjoyed freedom of religion. It was a very precious period. During that time, even though State and religions did not form an alliance, a trend in that direction began to emerge.

In the Christian world, the departure of the foreign missionaries raised many questions. Who should own and run properties and facilities like church buildings, missionary hospitals and missionary schools which were previously owned and run by foreign missionary agencies? As an atheistic political party, the Communist Party was suspicious of Christianity, which had always been associated with imperialism. They were looking for an appropriate opportunity and time to make their mark on religious affairs.

Birds of a feather flock together. The Communists did not take the initiative to approach religious leaders, but some religious leaders tried to approach the government. This development was to push the Christian world in China into an unprecedented era. People began to emerge on the stage of Chinese Church history who would later play an important part in influencing the development of China's policy on religions. One of them was Mr Wu YaoZong.

Wu YaoZong was born into a non-Christian family in Guangdong in 1893. After his conversion to Christ in 1918, he continued his studies at the Union Theological Seminary in New York and was subsequently taught by Niebuhr. He was trained as a liberal theologian, which means he did not believe in the virgin birth, a literal resurrection, the Trinity, Judgement Day, the second coming of Christ, or any doctrines he found unreasonable. In 1937, Wu YaoZong joined the Chinese Defence Alliance, which was organised by the Communists. His job was to collect medical equipment for the Eight-Path Army. He was a pro-Communist, left-wing Christian. His pro-Communist thought was apparent even in the titles of his articles. For example, he published an article entitled 'The Communist Party has Educated Me' in the magazine *Heavenly Wind* on 7 July 1951. In the article he wrote:

> 'In the past thirty years, I have experienced two major changes in my thought. Firstly, my conversion to Christianity – from religious scepticism to faith. Secondly, my acceptance of the anti-religion philosophy of materialism, and blending of it with religious belief.'

Wu YaoZong attended the Chinese People's Political Negotiation Conference on 2 September 1949 as one of the five representatives of Christianity. However, these five representatives were not chosen by Christian organisations. In November 1949, the Christian Visitation Team was set up under the leadership of Wu YaoZong. In May 1950, after visiting Beijing, the Team met Zhou EnLai on 2, 6 and 13 May. The thrust of their discussions was that Christianity should stamp out from itself all elements of imperialism. As early as 1950, the Communist Party had already fixed the direction of the development of Christianity. Their policy would, however, be implemented through recognised Christian leaders. The two immediate tasks of the Christian Church in China were, first, to break away from the imperialists and, second, to implement the Three-Self Movement, viz. to be self-governing, self-propagating and self-supporting.

On 8 July 1950, Wu YaoZong, together with the other leaders, launched a nationwide movement. They distributed an open letter entitled 'Declaration on the Means of Chinese Christians to Strive in the Building of New China' with a request for signatures to be gathered in support of this new direction. The Three-Self Patriotic Movement was thus launched officially. The Declaration stated the Church's new task: 'The Christian churches and organisations in China are to support the common guiding principles and, under the leadership of the government, are opposed to imperialism, feudalism and bureaucratic capitalism, so as to strive towards an independent, democratic, peaceful, unified and prosperous new China.' Through this Declaration, religion and the State were officially linked.

According to the official statistics announced by the Chinese government in August 1950, the Christian population in China was composed of approximately 3 million Roman Catholics – 80 per cent of them were in the villages – and approximately 700,000 Protestant Christians – 70 per cent of them in the villages.

On 13 September 1950, the 'Declaration of Reform' or 'Declaration on the means of Chinese Christians to Strive in the Building of New China' was announced. On the same day, *The People's Daily* published an article entitled 'The Christian Patriotic Movement', propagating the Three-Self Movement.

On 18 October 1950, the Chinese Christian Association held its fourteenth annual general meeting in Shanghai. The meeting approved the Three-Self Movement and Wu YaoZong was elected as the vice president. From then on, Wu YaoZong officially moved into the leadership of the Christian world in China.

In this period, the Three-Self Movement was still in its inception and ideological stage. Originally, its leaders planned to unify its leadership throughout the whole country in five years. However, something happened to accelerate the process.

On 25 June 1950, the Korean War erupted. On 27 June, the US intervened and on 27 July the UN also became involved. On 25 October, China went to the aid of North Korea by confronting the US. The Three-Self Movement made use of the Korean War to expedite its reformation, and from this time Christians began to be 'forced' into the Three-Self Movement. Anyone who did not join the Three-Self Movement was deemed to be supporting imperialism and became a traitor, or worse still, a counter-revolutionary. So a Christian was either a member of the Three-Self Movement or a supporter of imperialism. The Three-Self Movement was, therefore, actually a political movement in religious disguise.

On 29 December 1950, the 'Guidelines for Dealing with the US-Aided Education, Relief Organisations and Religious Organisations' were announced at the Sixty-fifth Conference of the Home Affairs Department of the Central People's Government. In April 1951, a meeting, attended by 154 representatives from all denominations and Christian organisations throughout the nation, was held to discuss how to deal with US-aided Christian organisations. Some of the representatives were church leaders who had nothing to do with the US missionary agencies. Compulsory membership of the Three-Self Movement was extended from foreign-aided churches to all churches. The conference spent two days denouncing the evil done by imperialists to Chinese churches. A nationwide Christian organisation was set up out of this conference: 'The Organising Committee for the Committee for the Chinese-Christian-anti-US-and-pro-North-Korea-Three-Self-Reformation Movement'. Wu YaoZong was elected as the chairman and Liu LiangMo as secretary. Wu YaoZong's position as the supreme leader of the Chinese Christian world was thus strengthened. This meeting also approved the 'Combined Declaration of the Representatives of Chinese Christians from Various Churches and Organisations' and the 'Draft of Measures to Deal with US-Aided Christian Organisations'. Both were officially announced by the Political Affairs Department on 24 July 1951. The Combined Declaration stated: 'Through the empowerment of God and the encouragement of the Communist Party, and under the leadership of Chairman Mao, Chinese churches as a community will develop a purer endeavour to serve the people.'

From that time Chinese churches entered into a period of accusation. *Heavenly Wind*, a Christian publication, abounded with articles like 'How to Lead an Accusation Meeting Well' and 'We Want to Indict'. Wu YaoZong and Liu LiangMo wrote many articles. They reinterpreted the doctrines of 'judgement' and 'regeneration' from the perspective of politics. Some Bible-believing Christians disapproved of and were critical towards their position, but, by September 1952, the Three-Self Movement had managed to collect more than 330,000 signatures.

In November 1951, the first cadre force of the Christian Three-Self Reformation Movement was trained in Shanghai, signalling the beginning of the movement to educate and remould believers.

Nevertheless, many Christians from all over the nation refused to join the Three-Self Movement. At that time there were about sixty Christian organisations in Beijing and eleven of them refused to join the Movement. They argued that they had always been self-governing, self-propagating and self-supporting, so they did not have to join. The leaders of these organisations and churches were: Wang MingDao, Yuan, Bi YongQin, Wang Zhen, Peng HongLiang, Wu MuJia, Wang WeiMing, Zhang ZhouXin, Chen ShanLi, Wu WenJing and Liu XiuYing.

Yuan repeatedly explained to the members of his church why he did not join the Movement. He had three major reasons. Firstly, his church had been self-governing since its inception in 1946. He had not joined any foreign missionary agency, nor had he attached himself to any organisation for support. Among the sixty or so churches in Beijing his was the only one renting premises for their meetings. Believers' offerings and his own part-time job of translation covered his entire family's livelihood and the rent of his church. Since it had always been self-governing, self-propagating and self-supporting, he did not need to join the Three-Self Movement. Secondly, he believed that Christ was the head of the Church; she belonged to God, and was pure. The Church should not form any worldly alliance. Church and State should be separated and people should give to God what belonged to God and to Caesar what belonged to Caesar. Politics should not tamper with religion, and Christian ministry should not rely on politics. Yuan disagreed with the government's policy of meddling in religious affairs through the Religious Affairs Bureau and seeing religious organisations as part of civil organisations that were meant to render their service to the government. Thirdly, he disagreed with the theological position of some of the Three-Self leaders. Yuan held to the conservative Evangelical view, and was opposed to Liberal theology. Though Wu YaoZong's theology recognised the existence of God, its concept of God was abstract. Yuan, however, believed in a living and personal God. Therefore, he always said, 'Believers and unbelievers should not be unequally yoked. This is a biblical teaching. Their God is different from ours. Therefore, we should stay away from them.'

Right from 1951, these eleven church leaders and their members had drawn the line at joining the Three-Self Movement. Yuan invited Wang MingDao to come and speak in his church once every month. The two men drew close to each other.

During this period, many believers came to Yuan with questions about whether they should join the Three-Self Movement. Once, a believer asked Yuan if he had read Liu LiangMo's article in the nineteenth issue of *Heavenly Wind* talking about his experience of being involved in politics. Liu equated this experience with Christian rebirth. He asked Yuan, 'Is this the new birth that Jesus told Nicodemus about?' Yuan told him, 'No. Being born again refers to receiving a new life after believing in Jesus. It's nothing to do with politics. It's only through the precious blood of Christ that we can receive forgiveness of sins and eternal life.' The leaders of the Three-Self Movement often published their articles in *Heavenly Wind*. These articles placed much emphasis on politics and revolution at the expense of spirituality. They tried to direct spiritual ministry through politics and revolution. Some of them were even purely political and were misguiding. Yuan told the believers, 'Don't read these articles. They offer no help for your spiritual life. You would do better to read Wang MingDao's articles in *Spiritual Food Quarterly* which make really worthwhile reading.'

Note

1. The Army Control Committee was a committee overseeing public order and security.

Chapter 10

'I Would Rather Suffer than Conform'

In 1952, the Three-Self Movement and the Chinese government began a series of initiatives to allure, persuade and
persecute those who refused to join the Movement. Through
the Three-Self Movement their intention was to bring all
Christians under the leadership of the Communist Party and
government. By the middle of 1952, they had succeeded in
luring large numbers of believers from the Nonconformist
churches into the Movement. The Nonconformists were
becoming increasingly isolated. A large number of believers
from Yuan's Gospel Hall deserted him but he was not at all
disturbed. He said, 'I'll shepherd whatever number of sheep
God entrusts to me. It's up to them to decide if they want
to join the Three-Self Movement. As for me, I choose not to
join.' In May 1953, the Christian Association decided to ban
the churches from inviting Wang MingDao, Wang Zhen
and Yuan to preach in their churches. The government
intended to force the eleven representatives who were
refusing to join to conform.

From 22 July to 6 August 1954, the first nationwide
Christian conference was held at the Methodist church in
Dengshikou, Beijing, at which Wu YaoZong gave a political
report. After the conference, he published 'An Open Letter
to Fellow Comrades', renamed the Three-Self Reformation
Movement as the Three-Self Patriotic Movement, and established a nationwide leadership, known as the Committee for

the Chinese Christian Three-Self Patriotic Movement, headed by himself. The leadership of the Movement was thus strengthened throughout the entire nation.

On 30 September 1954, in another attempt to persuade them, the Beijing local government invited more than 100 representatives from the eleven Christian organisations and churches which refused to join the Three-Self Movement to a meeting at the conference hall behind Zhongshan hall in Zhongshan garden. The meeting began with a speech by the chairman of the Religious Affairs Bureau, Mr Li, trying to persuade them to join the Three-Self Movement. After his speech, Mr Wang MingDao explained why he refused to join the Movement, as did some of the other participants. They were quite outspoken. Their reasons were: firstly, they had always been 'three-self', so they did not have to join, and, secondly, they were all Fundamentalists, with very different beliefs to those of the Three-Self leadership. Mr Wang MingDao referred to the Liberal camp as the unbelief camp. This was the first occasion on which both sides expressed their views. The meeting did not turn out as the government had expected, but at least they now knew why these Nonconformists were refusing to join the Movement. At the end of the meeting, the government gave every participant a copy of a book accusing the Americans of imperialism.

Following that meeting, the government realised that it was quite unlikely that these eleven Christian bodies would join the Three-Self Movement but they were not willing to leave it at that. Shortly afterwards, they came up with a new proposal. They wanted the members of these eleven bodies to attend political classes organised by the government. Since the Nonconformist leaders would clearly not be willing to study under teachers from the Three-Self Movement because of their different beliefs, the government compromised by proposing a new association in which they could study politics directly under government teachers. It was evident to the eleven dissenting leaders that the government's proposal was clearly aimed at them, but it was quite difficult for them to know how to respond. They were unwilling to attend these classes because, in their minds, politics and religion must be kept separate.

One day, Peng HongLiang from the Dongdadi Gospel Hall called in to see Yuan. He asked Yuan, 'Have you received the government's letter asking us to attend separate political classes?' Yuan replied, 'Yes, I have. I'm still wondering about how to respond.' Peng HongLiang said, 'Let's get together and discuss this. Why don't you send some postcards out, arranging a meeting at Wang MingDao's place so that we can reply to the government as soon as possible.' So, Yuan sent the postcards to the eleven leaders, arranging the meeting at Wang MingDao's place at 3.00 p.m. on a certain day.

On that day, the leaders of all the eleven groups turned up. After Yuan had briefed them on the purpose of the meeting, Wang Zhen said, 'I don't think we should attend these political classes. We must avoid being associated with the Three-Self Movement. Doves flying in two different flocks in the air will end up in one flock.' Other people expressed their agreement with him. They came to the conclusion that, if anyone was interested, he should attend as a citizen, not as a pastor or under the name of any church or Christian organisation. If they attended the classes as citizens, the government would not send their officials to teach them. In this way they subtly rejected the government's proposal.

The government still did not give up in their attempts to persuade them. In the latter half of 1955, Yuan received an invitation from Beijing's Religious Affairs Bureau to a banquet at Xinqiao restaurant on 26 January. He did not know that the Three-Self leaders would be there or that Wang MingDao had not been invited. He decided that it was not a big deal and he would go. When he arrived Mr Li welcomed him and shook his hand warmly, inviting Yuan to sit beside him. Yuan soon realised that the Three-Self leaders were there and that he was the only leader from the eleven Non-conformist groups present. He wondered whether he should leave, but he still thought that it was only a dinner and as such not a big deal – he felt it would be rather rude if he left halfway. Since he did not want to be thought a petty person, he stayed. Actually, some of the other Nonconformist leaders had planned to attend, but somehow got wind of the fact that the Three-Self leaders would be there, so they turned back en route.

During the banquet, Mr Li said, 'We're all men of faith. You can choose whether or not you wish to drink.' He was very friendly towards Yuan, asking about his family, and kept serving him with food and drink. He also toasted Yuan. He drank wine, while Yuan drank tea. The Three-Self leaders were also friendly towards him. Although Yuan had attended the banquet accidentally, Mr Li and the others took it as a sign of his potential acceptance of the Three-Self Movement. That is why they were extra friendly towards him. Mr Li said to Yuan, 'You're only forty or so and are still young. You should keep learning and keep progressing.' In other words, Mr Li thought that Yuan was still redeemable. This was probably why Yuan was spared when Wang MingDao was arrested for the first time in 1955, and also probably why they were willing to overlook Yuan's sending out postcards to arrange a meeting. They took the fact that Yuan had attended the dinner as a favourable indication and gave him more time to rethink his position.

In May 1955, the government began to impose coercive measures on the Nonconformists. Every day news reached Beijing of the many Nonconformists being arrested outside the city. The government was still hoping to persuade these eleven groups to join the Three-Self Movement, so they placed Beijing at the bottom of their list for coercion. But contrary to all expectations on 7 August, Mr and Mrs Wang MingDao were arrested, together with more than ten other pastors and believers from Beijing. This was the straw that broke the camel's back.

When a believer told Yuan about the arrest of Mr and Mrs Wang, he thought he was the next on the list. Facing these unprecedented pressures, Yuan's faith and ministry entered a period of depression. The government continued to use all sorts of means to persuade, threaten, and coerce the remaining leaders. In 1956, they finally succeeded in getting all the pastors in Beijing to attend political classes. They did not achieve this easily. They had been working towards this goal since 1953, and eventually attained it by combining persuasion with coercion. Yuan began to attend political classes in 1956 and he was taught directly by Mr Li. The content of the classes included the policies of the Communist Party, and how a church could work with the Party to build up the country. The Three-Self leaders and the government officials knew Yuan, so they had him sit in the first row in every class. It was on the one hand a way of expressing their 'concern' for him and on the other hand of observing his response. During the classes, Yuan kept quiet, for he did not know what to say. He was afraid that he might either say something that upset the government or else compromise his conscience. So he preferred to keep quiet.

During this period, Yuan battled with whether to continue to attend these political classes. For him, it was a struggle between the flesh and God's will. It made him withdrawn and caused him to re-evaluate everything he had done in the past.

Eventually, one day after his prayertime, he told his wife excitedly that he would not be attending the political classes any more. He was so happy he sang like a child again and his depression disappeared. HuiZhen could really feel for her husband. She had seen how much pressure Yuan had been under throughout this period. She could not resolve his problems but, now that he had made up his mind and was feeling such relief, she supported his decision. She thought, 'If he really doesn't want to go, he might as well not go; we haven't committed any crime so the government can't do anything to us.'

In 1957, the anti-right-wing struggle began. Yuan was invited to one of the mass political conferences organised by the Three-Self Movement. During the first few days of the conference, presided over by Mr Li, Yuan was very reticent to say anything. After a while, Mr Li said, 'Yuan, it's high time you said something. Why are you so quiet?' Yuan said, 'I've nothing to say. Let the others speak.' Mr Li said, 'Don't worry, say whatever's on your mind. Tell us what you think. Come on, it's no big deal.' Actually, Mr Li knew that Yuan had been reluctant to attend the conference, but had had no choice. He thought Yuan might be bottling up his grievances and wanted to know what was on his mind. So he encouraged Yuan, 'Come on, tell us what you think. We need your opinions and suggestions for improvements. If we have any shortcomings, we'll work on them.' Yuan quietly considered for a moment and then decided to say something. He had been bottling up his feelings far too long.

He said, 'Firstly, the government policy on religions is unfair. Christianity and Islam are treated unequally. The government's restrictions on Christianity are stricter than on Islam. Christians have almost lost their freedom of religion. Secondly, some of those in the Three-Self Movement are not "three-self" at all. They are those who sided with the Japanese during the Japanese occupation, turned to the Americans for support when they arrived in China and now have wangled their way into the Three-Self Movement. They are not "three-self" at all. They are impostors disguised as Christians in order to have full stomachs.'

After his speech, there was silence in the conference hall. Mr Li did not say anything. Now that he had poured out his grievances Yuan felt a great sense of relief. He thought, 'Why was I so stupid? It feels so good to pour out what's been in my heart. Why didn't I do that earlier? If I had spoken out earlier, I wouldn't have had to go through all this agony. I'll say it straight out in future.'

At the end of the conference, Yuan's group leader, Wang YiHua, announced, 'The government quota specifies that every group should produce four right-wingers. According to the speeches recorded, Yuan will be categorised as one of them.' He further explained, 'The right-wingers are dissidents, but instead of feeling disappointed, they should work harder and search their souls regularly.'

On hearing this, Yuan made no comment. At home, he told HuiZhen calmly, 'From today onwards, I'm a right-winger.' HuiZhen asked anxiously, 'Is there any punishment for right-wingers?' Yuan replied, 'We are required to search our soul. It's time for me to reflect quietly before the Lord.'

From this point on Yuan stopped attending the Three-Self classes. They sent for him a few times, but he refused to go, and eventually they tired of doing so. 'Three-Self' seemed to have disappeared from his life. He continued his normal daily life of praying and reading the Bible early in the morning and having three meetings a week, helping his children with their studies and studying the Bible until late at night. His life seemed to have gone back to its normal routine before 1953. Everything seemed to be going so smoothly.

Yuan referred to the current situation in most of his three sermons a week. He preached from the Bible on topics such as the characteristics of the church and of a servant after God's heart. He clearly stated, 'The Church should not be under the leadership of the Religious Affairs Bureau, or the Three-Self Movement. Christ is the head of the Church. We Christians have the right to refuse to participate in activities run by the Religious Affairs Bureau, which is a politically motivated organisation. This does not mean that Christians have any grievances against the government or the Party. Christ, not the head of the Religious Affairs Bureau or any so-called pastor, is the head of the Church. Religion and politics are two different things. Joining the Three-Self Movement should also not be equated with patriotism. Christians can participate in political activities, as long as they do not do it under the name of any church. The church is not a civil organisation. It is a heavenly and spiritual body.'

Many times after the meeting, Christians would approach Yuan and remind him, 'Pastor Yuan, you'd better be extra careful. I saw some strangers in today's meeting.' Yuan would say, 'Don't worry, the gospel is aimed at strangers. As long as a person is interested, the door is always open for him. I preached from the Bible. Some have strayed away because they don't know the teaching of the Bible.'

One day Pastor Qi TingDuo came to the Gospel Hall to see Yuan. After they had exchanged the usual pleasantries it was obvious that he wanted to say something to Yuan, but he could not seem to get the words out. It was time for lunch, so

Yuan invited him to have lunch together. Pastor Qi TingDuo had been on good terms with Yuan until he had begun to participate actively in the Three-Self Movement. Since then they had hardly kept in touch at all. As they were talking over the lunch table. Pastor Qi TingDuo kept sighing and eventually said, 'Brother Yuan, I've some advice for you. You probably won't like it, but I will still say it anyway. I've heard that you've stopped attending the political classes. This is very dangerous. You'd do well to exercise some restraint on your own preferences and pretend to learn their lessons. If you still insist on not joining the Three-Self Movement, you might bring trouble on yourself and your family. If something happened to you, whom would they turn to?' Tears ran down Pastor Qi TingDuo's cheeks. Yuan was not sure if he had been sent by the Three-Self hierarchy or was just giving advice off his own back. However, he knew that he was sincere and was thankful for his warning. But he could not agree with him. He said, 'I did not stop attending the classes because of my own preferences. I dare not fool God and I'm not willing to fool man.'

On another occasion Yuan was visiting a sick neighbour called Mr Wang and was just on the point of leaving when Pastor Qi TingDuo arrived, followed him out of the house, and started trying to persuade him to join the Three-Self Movement. He said, 'In the words of the ancient saying, "If we live under a low roof, won't we condescend?" [In other words, since we're under their authority, have we any choice except to give in?] We really have no choice. The Communist Party wants us to join the Three-Self Movement, so have we any choice?' Yuan did not say anything. He said to himself in his heart, 'We've ended up in today's situation because there are too many cowards. You are under their authority, but I'm not. I won't give in.'

After these two encounters with Pastor Qi TingDuo, Yuan knew that the government was not going to let him go. Pastor Qi TingDuo was right. If he refused to join the Three-Self Movement, he was asking for trouble. He did not know what was in store for him, but he could sense that catastrophe was imminent.

In November 1957, Beijing was in deep autumn, which was its most beautiful season, and the yellowish almond leaves were scattering all over in the wind. The beauty permeated the entire city. Yuan said to his wife, 'We haven't been to the Great Wall. Since the weather is so nice at the moment, let's take a trip there.'

As a pastor's wife, HuiZhen had to take care of their six children besides helping with Yuan's ministry. She was so overworked that she had strained her back. Yuan was also very busy. They had not been to the Great Wall although they had lived in Beijing for quite a long time. It was a good idea, but HuiZhen did not want to waste time. She said, 'Why don't we go another time? I've got to work round the clock making woollen clothes for the children.' Yuan said, 'Come on, I want your company. I haven't taken you out on a trip since you married me.' HuiZhen said, 'Why are you so keen to go now?' Yuan said, 'I'm leaving soon. We might not have this opportunity in the future.' HuiZhen was puzzled, but seeing that Yuan was so serious, she said nothing more and nodded.

This was the first time that he expressed his premonition (that something might happen to him).

At the end of 1957, HuiZhen received a call from Mr Li's secretary, asking her to go with Yuan's mother to Mr Li's office the next morning at 9 o'clock. He told her that Mr Li had a very important matter to discuss with them. His office was situated in the Religious Affairs Bureau in Chang'an Street. After talking it over, HuiZhen and her mother-in-law decided not to tell Yuan about it until after they had met Mr Li, so that he would not be worried. The next morning, HuiZhen and her mother-in-law went to the Religious Affairs Bureau after breakfast. Mr Li talked to them in his office for about an hour. He attempted to persuade them to use their influence with Yuan, to get him to align himself with the government. He was very serious. He said, 'I've arranged this meeting because I've got something to tell you, which is of the utmost importance to you. Yuan has not been attending the classes and he has not aligned himself with the government. I want you to persuade him to side with the government as soon as possible. Otherwise, we won't put up with this any longer. He is still young, only forty-four, and therefore he is still redeemable. That's why I arranged this meeting. You are the people closest to him, so you should try and persuade him. You have six young children and a senior member of the family to take care of. What will come of them if something happens to him?' We'll provide a way out, if Yuan repents, aligns himself with the government and attends the classes. Otherwise, we'll do to him what we've done to Wang MingDao. We've been giving him chances, waiting for him to change his mind. But we can't wait forever. If he is still unrepentant, we'll take action. We've been very kind to him. Believe it or not, you wait and see. It's easy for us to deal with him. But if he's imprisoned, what will come of your whole family? You're his wife, so you should persuade him. Don't try to defy the government, otherwise, you'll reap what you sow.' Mr Li said to Yuan's mother, 'Madam, I know that he is your only son. If he's gone, what will come of you? You should persuade him to attend the classes, align himself with the government and join the Three-Self Movement. It's for your own good. Remember, if he repents, he still has a way out. Otherwise, he'll have only himself to blame.'

The meeting had lasted just under an hour. HuiZhen and her mother-in-law did not say a word on their way home. They knew that the situation had come to a head. They arrived at home at about 11.00 a.m. HuiZhen prepared lunch for the children before they went to school. After the older ones had gone to school and the younger ones had gone to sleep, HuiZhen went to find Yuan. He was reading. Looking at him, HuiZhen suddenly felt a surge of sadness. She was wondering whether she should tell him about what had happened that morning when he asked, 'What's wrong?' HuiZhen said, 'Mr Li asked to see mother and me this morning.' Yuan was stunned. After a while, he asked, 'What did you talk about?' HuiZhen said, 'He wanted us to persuade you to join the Three-Self Movement and align yourself with the government.' Yuan said, 'Was it arranged by the government?' HuiZhen nodded. Yuan asked again, 'You went with mother?' Again she said yes. Yuan understood that, with this final ultimatum which threatened the survival of his family, the struggle was reaching its final climax.

The house was deadly silent. Yuan tried to continue reading but he could not concentrate any more. After a long silence, he sighed and said, 'I would rather suffer than conform.'

Yuan had now been completely freed from the shackles of fear and cowardice. Suddenly it seemed as if the sky cleared for him. His faith was strengthened, and his relationship with God stepped up a gear. He told HuiZhen, 'Cowardice is a sin to God. Man was bound by this sin in his weakness. That was why God said to Joshua, *"Be strong and courageous. Do not be terrified; do not be discouraged, for the Lord your God will be with you wherever you go."* [1] We should also be strong and courageous. We've gone through so many difficulties in the past. I don't believe God will give us a burden we are unable to bear. If we pray constantly and rely on Him wholeheartedly, He will surely protect us.'

The danger was approaching. One day, after Yuan had preached his sermon, a car stopped at the church and a few policemen [2] came in and arrested a believer by the name of Ha WenLi. This was also meant to be a warning to Yuan. Later, Guo Sun HuiQing, Yuan's co-worker since 1934, was also arrested. The government was showing its muscle through all these events. Yuan knew their intention. He told HuiZhen, 'A Christian looking forward to the rewards in heaven should not be bothered about what happens on earth.'

During this period, Yuan had on the one hand prepared himself for his arrest, but believed on the other that God would deliver him from this provided he had faith. But he had forgotten that God's ways are higher than man's ways and that God's thoughts are higher than man's thoughts. Neither can man know His plan or understand His will.

At night, Yuan could not sleep. He read the Book of Job over and over again. Job's words were a great encouragement to him,

*'I know that my Redeemer lives, and that in the end he will
stand upon the earth. And after my skin has been destroyed,
yet in my flesh I will see God.'*   (Job 19:25)

In the darkness, God's servant uttered his deepest prayer, 'O
God, whatever circumstances I face, I'm deeply convinced
that my Redeemer lives. Protect my heart and my mind,
so that they will be in You.'

Notes

1.   Joshua 1:9.
2.   Literally public security officers.

Photos

Mr and Mrs Allen Yuan at their residence
of the White Pagoda Temple in Beijing, 17 October 1999.

Allen Yuan and family in Beijing, 22 September 1997.

Allen Yuan [left] with his lecturer and classmate at the Far Eastern Theological Seminary (1934).

Allen Yuan's children at Fuchengmen Street, Beijing, 1951.

The Fuchengmen Gospel Hall in Beijing
(taken when Zhitianjinxiong visited the palace on 1 May 1957).

Yuan with his wife before his arrest (1957).

First photograph taken after Yuan's arrest (1959).

Yuan's wife and six children (taken after his arrest in 1959, Beijing).

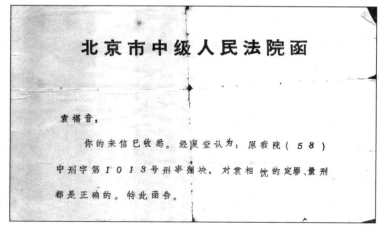

Letter from the Intermediate People's Court of Beijing answering
Yuan FuYin's inquiry about his father's release.

House meeting at Yuan's residence.

Prayer meeting.

With Mr Wang MingDao in Shanghai (1989).

With Mr Arnulf Solvoll [first from left], and his friends from Norway.

Billy Graham preached at Yuan's house-meeting in 1994.

With his co-workers in Shenshahai, Beijing, August 1997.

Celebrating their 60th wedding anniversary on 23 July 1998 in Beijing.

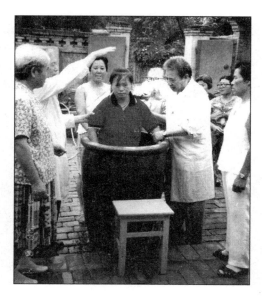

Baptising a villager.

Baptising 361 believers in a swimming pool in Beijing (1998).

Baptising in a suburban river (1999).

Mr and Mrs John Pattee,
missionaries from the Church of the Nazarene, USA.

Ann Xiao and her daughter Xiao YuPing.

With Miss Asta Nilson,
a missionary to China and Hong Kong from Sweden.

PART V

*'When he has tested me,
I shall come forth as gold'*

Chapter 11

Arrested

In 1958 spring arrived very late in Beijing. After Qingming, the first downpour of rain refreshed the city. Every morning Yuan took his youngest child, XiaoLiu, to eat breakfast at a food stall by the roadside. His six-year-old daughter became even more active during springtime. Being together with his daughter, Yuan felt the vitality of life, and the comfort of being a parent. But inwardly he did not feel relaxed. He knew that he would soon have to leave the family and he wanted to cherish these last moments.

It was very hot. Yuan changed out of his cotton clothes into his woollen ones. After HuiZhen had washed them, she wanted to put the cotton clothes of the whole family away. Yuan said to his wife, 'Don't put my cotton clothes away. Put them beside my pillow.' HuiZhen asked, 'Are you still going to wear them? If not, I'd like to put them away. I've just washed them and I'm afraid they will collect dust.' Yuan hesitated for a moment and then said, 'Wrap them in a cloth and put them beside my pillow.' HuiZhen did not say anything else. She piled up the cotton clothes neatly and wrapped them with a clean cloth. Then she put them beside Yuan's pillow.

Yuan perceived through his sixth sense that he was going to be arrested shortly. He was getting his cotton clothes ready so that he could take them with him when he was arrested. He had heard that the blanket in the prison was very thin, so he would need his cotton clothes. Two days later, Yuan said to HuiZhen, 'Buy a new pair of fabric shoes for me. Get a hard-wearing pair that will fit my feet well.' HuiZhen asked him, 'Why are you thinking of buying a new pair of fabric shoes?' Yuan usually wore leather shoes when he preached. Being a thrifty man, Yuan would only ask HuiZhen to buy him new clothes and shoes when they were torn or worn. If HuiZhen bought some new clothes for him when nothing was wrong with the old ones, he would rebuke her for being wasteful. Throughout these years, HuiZhen had got to know her husband's idiosyncrasies, and had been influenced by his carefulness. She was quite surprised that he had taken the initiative to ask her to buy a new pair of shoes for him. Yuan replied, 'I'm getting these fabric shoes for future use in a corrective work order.' On hearing this, HuiZhen was stunned. Now she understood that what Yuan had been doing was all in preparation for his arrest. She was dumbfounded and had to fight back her tears. Yuan also had to fight back tears when he saw his wife's distress. He acted as if he had not noticed and went out to read his book.

As his premonition of his arrest got stronger, he became more and more worried. He was not worrying for himself, but for his family. His mother was approaching sixty, and HuiZhen was unemployed. He had six children under his care. FuYin, the eldest son, had just reached seventeen while the youngest was only six years old. Five of them were still at school. The children in the family and his elderly mother all needed his care. As the head of the family, if he was gone, what would become of them all?

Satan knows just how to attack people. He knew Yuan's commitment to his family, and at the darkest moments of his journey of faith had repeatedly attacked this weak point. The warnings from the government as well as well-meaning advice from fellow believers all focused on this question: what will become of your family if you are gone? Today, he was facing this same challenge again.

The weakness was there. How was he going to overcome it? He was thinking very hard.

On the surface, there were only two options. Option 1: to give in to the government and join the Three-Self Movement. If he took this option, he would not be arrested and would not be separated from his family. Option 2: to insist on not joining the Three-Self Movement. If he took this one, he would certainly be arrested and would not be able to take care of his family.

Was there a third alternative? Yuan wanted to ask God to deliver him from this dilemma so that he would not have to defy the will of God by joining the Three-Self Movement while being kept from arrest and separation from his family. If God were to grant his request, he would continue to serve God in this Gospel Hall. He brought his request to the Lord in prayer. He asked God to make a way for him and his family. He also asked God to make a way for the evangelisation of China. He believed that God would grant his prayer if it came out of love for Him.

Of course God would protect the righteous. But he forgot that God had the right to protect His children in whatever way He chose. His ways are not our ways. When Yuan looked back on his arrest many years later, he understood that God had made a way for him, his family, Chinese churches and the evangelisation of China. In every area God exceeded what he had asked or imagined.

After more than ten days of prayer, Yuan experienced an increasing feeling of inner peace. Outwardly, there was also peace. No one warned or persuaded him. He thought that God had already answered his prayer and was going to deliver him from this trouble. He thought that God was going to make a new way for the Chinese Church so that people might see that it was all right not to join the Three-Self Movement. As long as Christians stood firm in their position, the government could do nothing to them.

On the morning of 19 April, HuiZhen returned from shopping. She gave a new pair of thick-heeled fabric shoes to Yuan, saying, 'Try them out first. See if they fit you.' Yuan was reading at that time. He did not lift his head and took the shoes absent-mindedly. When he was trying on the shoes, he suddenly recalled that he had asked her to buy these for him in preparation for his arrest. When Yuan did not say anything, HuiZhen thought that he was scrutinising the shoes, so she said, 'The shoes are very hardwearing. They cost $4.80. I took $10 and here is the change, $5.20. Let me put it in your pocket.' She stuffed the money inside his pocket. Little did they know that Yuan would be wearing these shoes and would have that $5.20 in his pocket in prison that same night.

In the history of China 1958 was an extraordinary year. During the spring, the central government issued a decree requiring the entire nation to participate in a campaign to eliminate four 'harms', one of which was sparrows. The method of eliminating the sparrows was quite unique. The whole nation was mobilised to create all kinds of noise to scare off and scatter the sparrows and keep them in the air until they were too tired to fly any more and eventually dropped dead. After the operation, the sparrow population decreased dramatically. There was, however, a disastrous consequence. From the next year onwards, without their natural enemy, insects increased exponentially, and this resulted in another kind of catastrophe. The crops were decimated leading to the great famine of 1959, which caused great suffering for the next three years. This is an illustration of the serious consequences of tampering with God's natural laws.

The killing of sparrows in Beijing was a well-planned operation. It was to begin at 9.00 a.m. on 20 April, and was well co-ordinated with the city divided into areas, the areas into divisions, and the divisions into streets. Everyone was required to participate in the operation punctually. On the night of 19 April, a street meeting was held to discuss the arrangements and, as the supervisor of the street, HuiZhen attended, returning home when it adjourned at 10.30 p.m. When HuiZhen arrived home, the children had already gone to bed and Yuan was lying in bed reading a book. Chen BangHeng, a blind young man, had come to talk to Yuan in the afternoon and after he had eaten dinner it was too late for him to get back, so he was also staying at the house that night. After washing up, HuiZhen was about to go to bed when she heard someone knocking on the door. A policeman yelled, 'Supervisor Liang, can you open the door, please?' She thought it was to do with the killing of the sparrows, so as she opened the door she asked, 'What's the matter?' She saw two men standing outside. She knew them quite well because they were from the police station in their street. They said, 'We're not looking for you. We're looking for Yuan. Our chief wants to talk to him.' Yuan said, 'OK, hold on a moment.' Yuan got up from his bed and put on his new pair of shoes. They were both expecting this, but as the policemen were so polite they did not think this could be the arrest. The fact was that the policemen, who had just participated in the street meeting together with HuiZhen, wanted to spare her from seeing her husband being arrested. As Yuan walked to the door, he turned back and cast a glance at HuiZhen, but did not say a word. Then he left with the policemen. Before leaving, one of the policemen said to HuiZhen, 'Go to sleep.' The other one said, 'We may be back later.' HuiZhen was puzzled, and wondered why they did not agree with each other. She also began to wonder why they wanted to take Yuan to the police station. Her heart began to pound heavily. She quickly knelt down and prayed. She could not sleep now.

As Yuan walked with the two policemen to the Xiang-jiayuan police station, he thought, 'Why have they summoned me? Does this mean that I'll never be home again?' He regretted that he had not said goodbye to his mother and his six children and that he had not passed on his work to any of his co-workers. One of the policemen asked Yuan, 'What counter-revolutionary organisation do you belong to?' Yuan was astonished. He said, 'I don't belong to any counter-revolutionary organisation. I'm not a coun-ter-revolutionary.' The policeman did not make any further comment. Actually, the government had already passed a verdict on him before his arrest: counter-revolution.

When they arrived at the Xiangjiayuan police station and sat down, three men whom Yuan did not know came into the room. They were probably from the city. They approached him and yelled at him brutally, 'Stand up!' Yuan stood up. One of them showed Yuan the warrant for his arrest and read it to him. After that, they took his thumbprint and handcuffed him. All this was completed within three to five minutes. The arrest was apparently well planned.

He was arrested at 11.30 p.m. on 19 April 1958. It was the beginning of Yuan's twenty-one years and eight months of imprisonment.

Half an hour after Yuan had been taken, HuiZhen was still praying when she heard the noise of many cars arriving at the house. 'Could it be that Yuan has been arrested?' she thought. She heard someone knocking at the door and when she opened it, she saw a number of policemen standing outside. One of them said to her, 'Yuan has been arrested. This is the warrant.' As he showed her the warrant, HuiZhen nearly fainted. But she said to herself in her heart, 'You must stand firm. Stand firm.' The policeman said, 'We want to do a thorough search of the house.' The policeman signalled to the others to begin their operation. About five or six police-men entered the house, holding tools in their hands. They began their search in the sanctuary of the church, hurling things all over the place.

The first to be awakened by the noise was Yuan's mother. On hearing that her son had been arrested, she began to tremble. HuiZhen said to her, 'Mum, let's go and wake up the children.' FuYin had already woken up. He was buttoning up his shirt as he walked out of the room. When he saw the pews, Bibles, hymnbooks, Christian literature and Yuan's drum scattered all over, he angrily ground his teeth. HuiZhen feared that he might easily do something impulsive, so she said to him, 'Go and wake up your brothers and sisters.' FuYin went in and woke them up. He also woke up BangHeng. The children were standing there with their sleepy eyes, looking at the policemen searching the house and wondering what was happening. The youngest daughter, who was still half-asleep when her brother took her out of the bedroom, was so frightened by all the commotion that she cried out, and this made all the others start to cry with her. HuiZhen cuddled her and patted her back. Standing beside her were her old mother-in-law and her children as they all watched the policemen searching their home.

After they had ransacked the sanctuary, they started on the other rooms. Each of them was holding a metal bar. With each step they took they banged it on the floor, searching for a cellar. After they had found the underground baptismal pool with nothing inside, they were still not satisfied and dug up the floor area around the pool. But they did not find anything. The search lasted from midnight to 4.00 a.m. When they had finished they loaded everything onto a truck and took it all away. Before they left, they said to HuiZhen, 'Do you think we've been reasonable in our search? If you think so, please sign here.' She did not look at what she was signing but just signed it. The policemen left at 4.30 a.m. HuiZhen's house no longer looked like their home. What a way to operate – searching before considering whether or not it was reasonable.

On the morning of 20 April, Chen BangHeng returned to the factory for the blind and gathered around him the brothers and sisters who went to Yuan's church. He told them, 'Pastor Yuan was arrested last night', and then he wept loudly. The others also wept.

At 9.00 a.m on 20 April, it was time for the operation to kill the sparrows. HuiZhen went to every house to gather people, as had been arranged the day before. The neighbours already knew that something had happened to HuiZhen's family, and they had not expected her to carry on as normal. They were very concerned about her but there was no way of showing it in the midst of this operation. HuiZhen was the street supervisor and presided over eleven resident committees. At that time, the Xiangjiayuan police station ran twenty-two residents committees, half of which were HuiZhen's responsibility. She was a volunteer and had accepted this job solely to help the neighbourhood. Even though her husband had been arrested, she still took her responsibility seriously and faithfully carried it out. She knew that this would be the last time she would act as the street supervisor. From the night of 19 April onwards, she had already been categorised as a member of a counter-revolutionary family. She was overwhelmed with grievances, questions, deep fears and anxieties, but she kept them bottled inside. She knew that Christians should be faithful to their duties. Whatever might happen in the future, she would still have to fulfil her job in the street and do it well today.

Among all the children, FuYin was the one most affected by his father's arrest. He was still studying in primary six, and was doing very well academically. Besides that, he treated his classmates very well and his teachers liked him very much. He had also been chosen as the leader of the young vanguard team. On the day Yuan was arrested, when FuYin came home from school, he had seen some men wearing blue sports shoes looking at his house. He thought something must have happened, and wondered what they doing. Although they were wearing sports shoes, they did not appear to be doing any exercise. They did not come from the neighbourhood and were just standing there. He did not know that his house was under surveillance.

His father's arrest had a deep impact on him. He did not fully understand why his father had been arrested, and did not know what would become of him as the eldest son of the family. On the day after his father's arrest, a poster with the words 'Down with Yuan' and a list of his offences was put up on the gate of FuYin's school. FuYin went to look at the poster after everyone had left in the afternoon. The same posters were also put up on the YMCA, Gangwa Temple and the White Pagoda Temple. After reading the poster, FuYin went around the city, looking for other posters. As Yuan's eldest son, he wanted to know why his father had been arrested. As he walked he kept looking around. After walking through the entire city, he found two kinds of posters against his father. One was written by the Three-Self leaders while the second was targeted against the key figures in the Nonconformist camp, like Wang MingDao and Yuan. Reading the posters, he was overwhelmed with emotion and wanted to run away. Yet he sensed an urge to turn back and finish reading. He did not believe that his father was a counter-revolutionary, but neither did he believe that the government would make an arrest without reason. He could not understand all these conflicting aspects of the situation, and he had no one to talk to – he did not want to upset his mother any more than she already was. With tears in his eyes, FuYin wandered the streets aimlessly. Doubts, bewilderment, despair and helplessness entered into the life of this seventeen-year-old young man prematurely, making him grow up overnight. He knew that from then on he needed to assume responsibility for the family.

A week later, his teacher called him into his office and informed him that his position as the leader of the young vanguard team would be handed over to another student. FuYin nodded, signifying acceptance, and did not ask the teacher why. The teacher did not tell him the reason for his dismissal, but it was obvious. When he came home, he did not tell his mother about this, because he did not want to worry her. He said to his mother, 'Mum, don't worry. I'll look for a job and take care of the family when I graduate in June.'

Chapter 12

Trials

During the time the policemen were searching Yuan's house, he was taken to Caolan Alley behind Beihai – a place where suspects were held before their trial – in a car. On arriving, one of the people in charge of the pre-trial unfastened his handcuffs and told him to squat in the corner. While the policemen and the pre-trial committee discussed Yuan's case Yuan did not say a word. At about 2.00 a.m., he was taken to a room for the night. The room was only about ten square metres, and already had more than ten people in it. Each of them slept on a plank-bed which was so narrow that it was impossible to turn over. A policeman pointed to an unoccupied plank-bed and told him to sleep there. After that, he left locking the door behind him. The other prisoners were awakened by the sound of the door opening and closing. Seeing a gentle-looking bespectacled middle-aged man, they did not say anything. Perhaps there were so many people coming and going that they had already become numbed to newcomers.

Lying on the plank-bed, Yuan could not sleep. His mind was in an uproar. He wondered if his family members knew where he was now, and what would become of him and his family. Everything was so uncertain. The thoughts kept going round and round in his head, getting nowhere. At seven o'clock the next morning, the warders brought in some food for breakfast. Each of them was given a *wotou* (steamed bread made of corn meal) and a bowl of cabbage soup. But

Yuan did not have any appetite. How could he eat at a moment like this? When he thought about it, he realised that he would need to be strong in order to be able to face his trial so he forced himself to eat a little bit. Each of them had been given only one chopstick instead of a pair and he wondered how they were going to eat with only one chopstick. But the others were gobbling up their food. So, with one chopstick, he ate the cabbage and drank the soup. He left the *wotou* on the plate and, before he could say anything, someone had already taken it. To this day Yuan could never understand why they were only given one chopstick.

According to the regulations of the pre-trial committee, each of the suspects was required to prepare for trial after they had washed and taken their breakfast every morning. Those who were summoned in the roll-call had to follow the soldiers while the rest stayed in the room. The roll-call started at eight o'clock every morning. On the morning of 20 April, Yuan was the first summoned. He was marched between two soldiers to a building set aside for trials and interrogated by three uniformed officials.

After asking for his personal details such as his name, age and place of origin, they interrogated him about the occasion when he had distributed postcards to arrange a meeting. The older man seated in the middle asked, 'Did you write and send postcards to gather people in Wang MingDao's church in Shijia Street for a meeting?' Yuan kept praying in his heart, 'O Lord, grant me wisdom to say the right words.' He nodded. They looked at each other; perhaps they were surprised that Yuan had admitted it so easily. He then asked, 'When did you write the postcards?' Yuan said, 'I've forgotten.' He was telling the truth, but the event had happened a long time ago. When he was sending out the postcards he had not paid much attention to the date. But they did not believe him and thought that he was being difficult, so they ordered him to answer honestly. They asked him whether he admitted to committing an offence by writing illegal letters to arrange a meeting. Yuan said, 'What I sent were postcards, even the postmen could read the contents. Nothing was meant to be secret. They were certainly not illegal. Furthermore, informing Christians about a meeting was not an offence at all.' On hearing this, the middle-aged man was furious. He threatened him and said that if he refused to own up, he should wait to see what happened. He thought they were going to resort to violence, but they only meant to frighten him. After that, they sent him back to 'search his soul'.

When he returned to his room, those who had not been summoned to trial asked him what had happened but Yuan did not say anything. Some of the older men told Yuan, 'You must own up, they will reduce your sentence if you own up.' Yuan said, 'Why should I own up? I've done nothing wrong!'

This trial was followed by a long series of other trials in which they asked a lot of detailed questions. This was an agony for Yuan, for he really could not remember all the details. It was not so much because he did not have a good memory as because he did not pay much attention to the details of daily living which were all taken care of by HuiZhen. He had focused all his attention on the ministry of the gospel. Therefore, during the interrogation, he kept having to give such answers as, 'I've forgotten', 'I don't know', and 'I've not committed any offence'. When they asked him why he could not remember, he told them that he was not in the habit of paying attention to such things, but the policemen accused him of resisting interrogation. So Yuan could only remain silent. After his release from the prison, he could not even remember most of the questions he had been asked during the interrogations. He could only remember that when the policemen asked him to repeat his right-wing remarks, he could only think of two – that he had said that Christianity had been unfairly treated and that he had accused some of the Three-Self leaders of going against the spirit of Three-Self. The policeman said, 'Why don't you own up to your third remark against Chairman Mao?' He was supposed to have said, 'Why doesn't the old monk say something?' Yuan was bewildered; he could not remember ever saying such a thing. He said, 'I really don't remember ever saying such a thing. My remarks which you label as right-wing were actually what you asked me to express freely in the conference, which I initially refused to do.' The policeman said, 'How were we going to know your counter-revolutionary ideas if we did not allow you to express your opinions? There has been an accusation that you referred to the Communist Party as the great red dragon and preached against patriotism and loyalty to the Party in your sermons.' Yuan said, 'I only preached from the Scriptures.'

The policemen also interrogated him concerning his slanderous remarks against the Three-Self leaders. Yuan, 'I did indeed make such remarks, but I was just stating the facts. As a Congregationalist pastor, Wang ZiZhong originally belonged to an American denomination. During the Japanese occupation, he became the leader of the Chinese Christian Fellowship. He was later appointed as the vice president of the Three-Self Movement. All Christians know this. Since this is a fact, I've not committed any offence in stating it.' The policemen also questioned him about a time when he escorted a Ms Hu JunDe to Guangzhou. Ms Hu had been a nurse in the Ophthalmology Department of the hospital and had worshipped at Yuan's Gospel Hall. Her husband had been doing business in the USA and, seeing that the situation in China was worsening, she had decided to leave too. In 1956, in order to catch a flight from Guangzhou to the USA with her twins, she had had to take a train from Beijing to Guangzhou. As she had a lot of luggage, she had asked Yuan to help her, and so Yuan had accompanied her to Guangzhou. When they had arrived in the city, it was already late in the evening, so they had stayed overnight at Mr Lin XianGao's house at Dama Station. Ms Hu had left China the next morning, and Yuan had taken the train back to Beijing. This had been Yuan's first meeting with Lin XianGao and, due to time constraints, he had not talked much with him. Referring to this incident the police charged him with collaborating with foreigners to commit treason. Yuan said that he had been merely helping his friend and since that occasion they had not had any further contact.

The police also interrogated him about his relationship with the Japanese pastor who had previously rented the

Gospel Hall. Yuan answered honestly, 'When I established the Gospel Hall in 1946, the Japanese pastor Oda Kaneo had already been sent to the concentration camp. I rented out the place directly from the landlord and did not contact Oda Kaneo. He was repatriated in the autumn of 1946. On Labour Day 1957, he was part of a team visiting Beijing. He visited the Gospel Hall, but the Three-Self Movement sent someone to accompany him. I did not know that he was coming. How could I collaborate with him? If there was any collaboration, it was between him and the Three-Self Movement.' But the police said, 'What we mean is that you collaborated with the Japanese before 1946.' Yuan replied, 'I returned to Beijing two months before the surrender of the Japanese in 1945 to visit my mother who was terminally ill. I stayed at home to take care of her, and Oda Kaneo was sent to the concentration camp two months later. How could I possibly have collaborated with him?' But the police said, 'No matter how many plausible arguments you come up with, you're still suspected of treason.'

In the course of the trials, the police made this remark about him: 'You're not answering any questions honestly and you are not willing to own up. When answering questions you always say that you have forgotten or deny committing any offence. Such behaviour is tantamount to resistance.' In order to punish him, they decided to send him for 'education', to give him the opportunity to 'search his soul'.

Yuan's fellow inmates came from a variety of backgrounds. The offences of the others were not as serious as those alleged against him. When he first arrived, he met a young Roman Catholic, with whom he naturally felt a sense of solidarity. This young man, who was only about twenty, was sent to jail because of his refusal to join the Roman Catholic Patriotic Committee. Sometimes he sat in a corner and sighed, and Yuan would go over and comfort him. He was afraid that he might be imprisoned for life and became very nervous before every trial. When Yuan learnt that he was only a lay person, he told him, 'Don't worry. You won't face any major problems. You're so young and have not committed any serious offence. They will release you after some sessions of interrogation. Actually, our situations are similar; we're being persecuted for righteousness. It's a religious matter, it's not a big deal. God is only testing our faithfulness through this little trial.' Yuan sincerely believed this. In the face of imminent catastrophe, Yuan still thought that this was only a religious matter. How naïve he was. He did not realise that his refusal to join the Three-Self Movement was tantamount to being unpatriotic and therefore counter-revolutionary. His offence was no longer merely a religious matter, but was considered counter-revolutionary.

After a few trials, the young Roman Catholic sensed from the indirect communication of the policemen that he had no major problems. His emotions began to settle down and he began to plan for his future after release. The young man was originally from Yunnan but had been arrested in Beijing. Yuan was worried that he might not have enough money to travel home, so he said to him, 'If you have any financial problems when you get out, go to my wife in my Gospel Hall. She's Ms Liang. Tell her that you're a Roman Catholic, she'll certainly help you.' After that he talked to him about the differences between Roman Catholicism and Protestantism and asked him to think about them. The young man reported this to the police the next day, telling them that Yuan had attempted to convert him and that he was still spreading his religion in prison. The police accused him of continuing his counter-revolutionary activities in prison and added this to his list of offences. In return for this, the young man was released within a few days.

After being betrayed by the Roman Catholic, Yuan became more cautious about what he said. Most of the time he would not talk; he would sit down quietly and meditate or pray. The inmates did not know his background and did not understand him. In fact, this was how God protected him from the violence among inmates that was a common feature of prison life.

The prison warders permitted and even encouraged violence among the inmates to 'help' particular individuals with their 'soul-searching'. There were basically three kinds of violence. The first and lightest was verbal criticism. The inmates would gang up on one of the prisoners and criticise and punish him by making him do some chores for them like folding blankets and cleaning chamber pots. In the second kind they would punish a fellow prisoner by making him sit up straight on the plank-bed with both his legs folded, for 'soul-searching'. Although not painful, it was very tiring. The one being punished would be forced to sit in this position for at least one hour, sometimes for the whole night. By the time he fell asleep, both his legs were numb. Sometimes, he became so exhausted that he fell off the plank-bed, but he would be forced to continue until his persecutors agreed to stop. The third form, which was the most severe, was nicknamed 'sitting on an aeroplane'. The victim's hands were lifted up and then pulled behind his back. Groans resulting from this punishment could be heard every night. The warders could clearly hear it, but they would not bother as they had actually instigated it.

Yuan seldom spoke in the jail. Even though he answered every question asked in the trials, the interrogators were never satisfied. The policemen arranged for him to be punished in the cell by his fellow prisoners. The warders explicitly and implicitly instructed the other inmates to torture Yuan but God protected him from serious injury. He was made to sit on the plank-bed for 'soul-searching'. Yuan did not understand why he did not suffer more severely. He could only thank God.

His greatest trial in prison was his longing for his family. Every evening, from the window of his cell he could hear the voices of children playing and he would think of his six children, fearing that they might be being bullied and worrying about their wellbeing and their future education. Whenever he smelled cooking, he would miss his wife's cooking. All these inner struggles raged inside him. His mother needed his care, his wife needed his support and his children needed his protection. On the one hand there was the pressure of his family's needs and on the other the difficult life in jail. These were his most vulnerable moments and could easily have lured him into looking backwards and falling. But he was continually reminded of the verse: *'No one who puts his hand to the plough and looks back is fit for service in the kingdom of God'* (Luke 9:62). Yuan was experiencing the pain of loving the Lord more than his parent and his children. But he was preserved by the Lord in his weakness.

Yuan also missed his co-workers. He was arrested on 19 April and, since visits were not allowed, he had lost contact with them. He was afraid that they would get into trouble because of their relationship with him. Since the launch of the Gospel Hall, Yuan had met with all his co-workers on the public holidays every 1 May and 1 October. After his arrest, he wondered if the church still had regular meetings and if his co-workers were still active in their service. Actually, the Gospel Hall had stopped meeting since his arrest and his co-workers had all scattered. However, he was not aware of this and could only pray for them.

During the series of trials, which lasted for half a year, Yuan was completely isolated from the world outside. He had lost touch with his family, his church and current affairs. All he had were his memories, orders from the police, accusations from inmates and demands to accuse others. Yuan told the police, 'I've got a poor memory. I can't even remember all the things that have happened to me. Whatever I can remember I've already told you. Concerning other matters, you'd better ask others, I really don't know.' Many of the cases of his inmates, including people arrested after him, had already been closed. His case could not be closed because he refused to confess. The police had repeatedly warned him that it was a serious offence to resist. But Yuan said, 'I have not refused to confess, because all the things you are accusing me of are not offences at all. I have not resisted. I'm telling the truth.'

In October 1958, after he had been in the jail for almost half a year, the court ordered him to write a confession. Yuan knew that they wanted to close the case. After he had written the confession, he was transferred to the prison in Zixin Road, Beijing, and thus he began his corrective work order. He was sent to work in the towel factory and then transferred to a sock factory. Every day, during his work in the sock factory, he saw prisoners receiving the announcement of their sentences. Some laughed, some wept, and some even fainted on the spot. Representatives from the court read the sentence out to the prisoners. When Yuan heard others' sentences, he began to calculate his own term of imprisonment. At that time, he still naively believed that his offence was on religious and not counter-revolutionary grounds.

Yuan was sentenced in November. When his sentence was announced to him by the court representative, he was working in the factory. He was sentenced to life imprisonment. The sentence book said that Yuan was a counter-revolutionary leader and, in addition, had showed a poor attitude in the trials by resisting. So he was punished severely. Yuan could not remember all the contents of the sentence book, except that he was allowed to appeal within ten days. He said, 'I won't appeal. Christians don't initiate lawsuits.'

Most of the inmates in the prison in Zixin Road fainted on the spot when they heard the sentence of life imprisonment. Yuan was one of the rare exceptions. The thought that he would be sentenced to life imprisonment had never even entered his heart because he always believed he had not committed any serious offence. He was not very sad when he heard the sentence. His attitude at the time was: there is no difference between staying one year in prison or a whole lifetime. After the trial of fire he had come through, he appeared before God and men as a strong man, who was prepared to be a martyr for the Lord at any time. He did not expect to walk out of the prison alive.

Yuan was ready to face his uncertain future; he only asked for an obedient heart. He did not realise, and could not know, that God had His good purpose for his imprisonment. He never realised that, had he not been arrested in 1958, he would already have been killed in the Cultural Revolution. Had he not been exercising physically through the corrective work order, he would been too weak to survive. In these most tumultuous years of Chinese history, God had sent His servant into a safe haven. Many died doing corrective orders in the field, but Yuan was spared. Throughout his twenty odd years in prison he never fell ill a single time. God worked miraculously in his life.

After Yuan's arrest in 1958, all the sixty-four churches in Beijing combined into four churches. In 1966, all the churches were closed down and the Communist Party achieved its goal of eliminating religion.

In the latter part of 1958, HuiZhen moved out of the Gospel Hall with her six children and her mother-in-law. She moved to a new house at 40 White Pagoda Temple Street, which originally belonged to the White Pagoda Temple. The lama rented it out until the government confiscated it. Eight of them squeezed into this small room which was only about ten metres square. All they had was a few bags of clothes. HuiZhen and the children went out and got some planks. They put the planks on top of some bricks and placed a mattress on top of them, and the whole family slept on this bed. At that time the family was very poor. After Yuan's arrest, HuiZhen found a job in the Housing Department, working as a construction worker. This job was physically exhausting with very low pay. No one was willing to work as a construction worker but HuiZhen thanked God that she had managed to get a job.

More painful and worrying for her than her own hard life was what was happening to Yuan. She also had to face her children's pain. Xiaoliu was still very young. She would cry whenever she thought of her father and kept asking, 'Where's Dad?' HuiZhen wanted to spare her from further hurt, so she told her that he had gone to attend political classes. Every day she waited for her father's return so that he would take her to eat fried liver at the stall across the street. Xiaoliu was very intelligent and articulate and Yuan loved her very much. She loved her father very much too and had wanted him to tell her stories every night. Yuan would carry her in his arms and tell her stories while he put her to bed. When she was asleep, he would lay her on the bed. Xiaoliu always asked her mother, 'Where's Dad? Why hasn't he returned after attending classes for so long? Why do my friends' fathers stay at home but Dad is always out?' HuiZhen fought back her tears and forced herself to smile as she comforted her child. She knew that she had to remain strong in order to support the family.

One morning in November, at about six o'clock, HuiZhen was still in bed when she heard someone knocking at the door. She answered quickly and found two strangers on the doorstep. They asked, 'Are you Ms Liang? Did you move from the Gospel Hall? Are you related to Yuan?' She answered yes to all their questions. She knew that they were going to give her some information about Yuan. One of them said, 'We're from the court. Yuan has been sentenced. Listen while I read the sentence to you. Afterwards I'll ask if you have understood.' So they told her that Yuan had been sentenced to life imprisonment. HuiZhen was stunned, but she told them that she understood. They handed her the sentence book and told her, 'You have ten days to appeal to the high court.' HuiZhen said, 'I won't appeal.' They said, 'OK.' They told her that Yuan was in the prison in Beijing and, now that the trials had ended, monthly visits were allowed. They told her that she would receive a postcard from Yuan telling her the visiting dates. Then they left.

After the delegates from the court had left, HuiZhen read the sentence book. Yuan was charged with seven offences:

1. Right-wing remarks.
2. Opposition to and tearing down the Three-Self Patriotic Movement and slandering its leaders.
3. Arranging an illegal meeting and resisting political classes.
4. Slandering the government on the grounds of limiting religious freedom.
5. Continuing counter-revolutionary activities in prison with a high-handed attitude.
6. Suspicion of treason.
7. Collaborating with foreign countries.

When other people heard about the sentence of life imprisonment, they said to HuiZhen, 'This sentence is too harsh. Why don't you appeal?' HuiZhen replied, 'All these are from the Lord. My husband did not commit any crimes such as robbery or theft. The Lord has permitted all these. As a Christian, I should not initiate any lawsuit. Now that he has been sentenced to life imprisonment, I can only submit.'

Chapter 13

Life in Prison – the Early Part

(The Prison in Beijing, Winter 1958–Summer 1960)

In December 1958, HuiZhen received her first postcard from Yuan in prison in Beijing, asking her to visit him on a certain day that month. When she saw his handwriting, tears streamed down her cheeks, but she was afraid that her mother-in-law or children might see her crying and become distressed, so she fought back her tears. On the Sunday of the visit, HuiZhen woke up early in the morning, bought some of Yuan's favourite foods and went with her mother-in-law and Xiaoliu to Zixin Street by bus.

When they arrived at the prison, Xiaoliu asked her mother, 'Mum, what is this place? Why are there high fences?' HuiZhen said, 'This is where your dad is attending classes.' She had always told her that her father had been attending political classes. When they walked to the gate, Xiaoliu saw the prison block and some soldiers with rifles, and she was afraid. So HuiZhen picked her up and carried her. When they arrived at a small black door, HuiZhen handed Yuan's postcard to the sentry and, after reading it, he let them in. There were crowds of people there, young and old, all waiting to be allowed in for their visit. They had to be taken in in batches. Each batch was given half an hour. HuiZhen, her mother-in-law and daughter queued up and waited for about an hour before it was their turn. A soldier took her postcard and told them to sit at a small desk. Then he brought out

Yuan. When she saw Yuan walking out through a small door, bald, skinny and pale, tears filled her eyes, but she told herself that she must not cry. When Yuan saw them, he quickened his pace and sat down at the desk. He held his mother's and wife's hands. After looking hard at him for a while, Xiaoliu finally recognised that this bald man was her father and shouted happily. Yuan touched her face. They were all very emotional and did not know what to say.

His mother broke the silence. She said, 'Everything at home is OK, don't worry. You must take care of your health here.' HuiZhen said, 'You must learn how to take care of yourself here. I've brought some of your favourite foods and clothes. If you need anything, write it on a postcard and send it to me.' Yuan reassured them, 'Everything is OK here. Don't worry. It doesn't matter if I suffer a bit physically as long as I feel inner joy and peace. As for the corrective work order, I've been assigned to work in a towel factory. Don't worry.' HuiZhen wanted to tell him about the arrest of some of his co-workers, but a guard was standing beside them all the time, so she could not risk it. She told him that they had moved to a house in White Pagoda Temple Street, that FuYin had entered Shougang Vocational School and would work in Shougang after two years, and that she had found a job on a construction site. Yuan asked her, 'Is your work on the construction site very tiring? Don't wear down your health.' HuiZhen said, 'Oh, it doesn't matter. I'm not too tired.' She took out a few packets of pastries for him but he told her that prisoners were not allowed to receive food. He said to his mother, 'Mum, now that I can't take care of you, you must take care of yourself.' She said, 'Don't worry. I'm well. HuiZhen's been very good to me. You've got to take care of yourself.' After half an hour, a policeman blew the whistle and Yuan had to leave.

This was their first meeting since Yuan's arrest. After being apart for half a year, Yuan had become thinner, but he was in good spirits. That comforted HuiZhen. After that, HuiZhen visited him every month. Each time she would take a different child with her so that he was able to see every one of them.

On one occasion, Mrs Xiao, his former teacher, visited him. He was overjoyed. He was not allowed to speak with her but could only nod to her signifying greeting. Xiao YuPing, Mrs Xiao's daughter, was also imprisoned in the Beijing prison at that time, but he did not see her, because men and women prisoners were separated. Actually, a prisoner seldom saw anyone other than the inmates of his cell.

According to the prison regulations, every prisoner was required to watch a film on the revolution in order to be re-educated. They were often forced to watch the same film so many times that they could even memorise the conversations. The film was shown in a field where a sheet of white cloth was set up as the screen. The prisoners carried a camp stool to the field to watch it. In one incident in 1959, as Yuan was carrying his camp stool to the field, he bumped into Wang MingDao. This was how he found out that Wang MingDao had been arrested again. They were not allowed to talk to each other, so they looked one another in the eye and then looked up to the sky, signifying looking up to the Lord. After they had understood each other, they nodded and moved on.

In an interesting incident Yuan also bumped into Zhang ZhouXin. The prisoners were allotted a specific period to go to the toilet. They had to go cell by cell, and more than ten prisoners from each cell queued up. Sometimes, prisoners from two different cells would bump into each other, but they were not allowed to talk to each other. The one in the toilet had to say his number out loud before he came out. One day when Yuan and his inmates were waiting outside the toilet, he heard someone shout 'No. 13'. He immediately thought, 'Could that be Zhang ZhouXin?' They had worked together from 1938 to 1939 and Yuan was very familiar with his accent. There were not many people with such a strong Fujian accent in the Beijing prison. When the man came out, he was indeed Zhang ZhouXin. They were surprised and nodded to each other. As they passed, they rubbed each other's shoulder, and Zhang ZhouXin nudged Yuan with his arm and stuffed a roll of toilet paper in his hand and walked away quickly. Meeting his old friend in such a place was very precious to Yuan.

Many prisoners wanted to curry favour with the prison authorities in a bid to reduce their term of imprisonment. The easiest way to achieve this was by exposing others. Yuan saw how some men who had been sentenced to more than ten years of imprisonment used these means to have their terms reduced. Because of this Yuan was very cautious with his words – he had already learnt his lesson. Generally, he would not talk to others, except those that he knew very well. Perhaps because he had already been sentenced to life imprisonment, most of the prisoners did not focus on him as a target for exposure. Yuan would never stoop to do anything like that. On the day he heard his sentence, he had already come to terms with the fact that he would grow old and die in the prison. He only asked God to help him to hold fast to His Word in all circumstances.

There was a young man in the prison who was originally a waiter in a guesthouse and had been imprisoned because he had stolen a camera from a foreigner. Although he had no previous record, stealing from a foreigner was considered a serious offence that would harm the nation's foreign relations. His term was reduced because he exposed another prisoner. He was, however, arrested again later, for he had learned some skills in prison and stole again when he was out. Apart from God's grace, nothing can save human beings.

Chapter 14

In Prison in the North-east
(Summer 1960–Autumn 1962)

In the summer of 1960, due to the increasing number of prisoners in the Beijing Prison, the government decided to transfer those serving terms of twenty years and above to Heilongjiang. Towards the end of the summer, Yuan was one of a number of prisoners who were sent by train to the Xingkaihu prison in the north-east region of Heilongjiang. Soldiers armed with machine guns were stationed at each end of the coaches to guard the prisoners. It was night-time when the train arrived at Shenyang station, and the prisoners were already starting to feel cold. When they arrived at Heilongjiang, the guards distributed cotton clothes and leather caps to each of them. More than ten Jeeps were already there waiting to take them to the prison. As the Jeeps passed through the streets, the children came out to see the prisoners and shouted, 'You're all counter-revolutionaries, you're all counter-revolutionaries!' In those days, even before the children learned how to read, they knew what a counter-revolutionary was. This was how tense the situation in China was at that time.

Xingkaihu was situated by the river at the border between China and Russia. When they first arrived, the prisoners lived in tents within a compound surrounded by barbed wire and guarded by armed soldiers. However, it was impossible to survive the winter in tents and their first task was to build a prison. Some of them were assigned to make bricks, while the others laid the bricks for the walls. After that they built houses for the warders and then they built their own prison cells. Each cell was 50 metres in length, with a heated brick platform for use as a bed and a stove under the platform burning coals or firewood. Each inmate's bed was very narrow. During the winter, the prisoners ate sorghum almost every day. They hardly had any vegetables. When the situation was better they sometimes had tofu. One Sunday a month they were given eight buns which was considered a very good meal. One of their major foods was potato – blackened potatoes. That was why, for many years after his release, Yuan didn't eat potatoes.

After they had built the prison, their major task was farming. They also collected grass for use as fuel. In this region the grass was abundant and grew taller than a man. It was the first time Yuan had ever seen such tall grass.

There were three treasures in the North-east: ginseng, marten fur and Wula grass. Before he left Beijing, HuiZhen had knitted woollen socks for him but these were nowhere near as warm as the Wula grass. The prisoners often went to collect Wula grass in winter; they would roll it up and stuff it inside their shoes. God's creation is indeed wonderful. God has prepared plants that match the climactic conditions.

It was so cold in that region that every drop of water immediately froze. Once when he was working, the temperature fell below −30°C. Someone saw that his nose turning white and told him to go inside the building immediately. Had he waited any longer, his nose would have frozen. It was said that frozen ears could be torn off and that people who had frozen to death were seen still standing and smiling. Although Yuan never witnessed anything like this, he often heard people telling stories about it.

Not long after he went to the North-east, it was the Mid-autumn Festival. At that time, the three-year famine had already begun as a result of the government's campaign to kill the sparrows and the prisoners only had *wowotou* to eat during the festival. In the spring of 1961, life in prison took a turn for the worse and they did not even have enough *wowotou*, so they had to look everywhere for wild vegetables to make vegetable *wotou*.

At that time, there were six farms for corrective work orders in Xingkaihu, and Yuan was working in the fourth division. Sometimes, some prisoners threw some *wotou* across the river to the Soviet Union and the people there threw back some bread as a friendly gesture. Some prisoners who could no longer stand the starvation ran across the border to the Soviet Union, only to be sent back later in a sack. They were not regarded as useful; worse still, they were treated like animals.

In 1962, following the incident at Zhenbao Island, China and the USSR broke off diplomatic relations and the Chinese government felt it was no longer appropriate to have its prisoners at the border so they decided to transfer them back. One day, to the prisoners' bewilderment, the chief warder said to them, 'You're going to be transferred back to Beijing.' A while ago they had been told that the prison in Beijing was full, but now they were being transferred back. But in such a difficult period, it would be better in Beijing than the North-east, so the prisoners were glad to return. On the return journey by train, in the autumn of 1962, everything was the same as on the outward journey except that they peeled off their clothes piece by piece as the weather became warmer.

The return to Beijing was unexpected good news for Yuan. Before they left, he could not wait to send a postcard to HuiZhen, informing her about his return. HuiZhen was overjoyed when she received the news. It was like a dream.

The train carrying more than two thousand prisoners stopped over at the corrective work order in Chadian, Tianjin, for lunch. Most of the prisoners were left there and only a minority sent back to Beijing.

When Yuan got off the train, he ran into an old friend, Yang JinGuang. Yang JinGuang, a Cantonese, became a Christian at Yuan's Gospel Hall while he was studying in Beijing. He was very zealous in the ministry and visited Yuan's house frequently. When Yuan had been arrested Yang JinGuang was still free. Yuan had mixed feelings when he saw him. On one hand he was glad to meet his old friend, but on the other he was sad to know that he had also been imprisoned. Yang JinGuang had been accused as a member of the Wang MingDao counter-revolutionary syndicate, and was serving his term of corrective work order in Chadian. Being prohibited from talking, they could only nod to each other.

At the stopover, each of the prisoners was given a bowl of vegetable soup. Yuan thought that it was the appetiser before the 'main course'; perhaps the warders were being considerate and knew that the prisoners needed something to quench their thirst before having their lunch. But no more food was served. During the famine, even the ordinary people were starving, so the prisoners were only given vegetable soup. Yuan got on the train with a hungry stomach but joyful heart. He was joyful because, being considered a dangerous prisoner who collaborated with foreigners, he was not permitted to stay in Chadian but had to be sent back to Beijing. He knew that this was the grace of God so that he could return to Beijing.

Chapter 15

Return to the Prison in Beijing
(Autumn 1962–Spring 1966)

It was good news for Yuan to be sent back to Beijing because it meant he could see his family more often. Furthermore, during the famine the food situation in Beijing was better than in many other places. The prison changed its regulations and allowed family members to bring food in to the prisoners. In the North-east, Yuan had eaten vegetable *wotou*, but later he only had chaff *wotou* to eat. After he returned to Beijing, all he had was dried sweet potatoes to eat. This was how difficult the situation was. However, Yuan did not suffer too much, because his family members brought food to him each month.

At every visit, HuiZhen would bring some pastries and sweets. Things were really difficult for the family in those days. Food was rationed and each member of the family only had 100 g of oil, 250 g of meat and 250 g of pastries each month. They would not use any of their pastries' allowance but save it all for Yuan. No matter what the situation was in the outside world at that time, Yuan was the best provided for of all the prisoners and was well nourished.

On visiting day, HuiZhen would wake up early in the morning and queue up to buy the pastries. In those days, there were not many goods in the shops and, even though she had a pastry voucher, she still had to queue up early in the morning because, if she were late, everything would be sold out. When she returned with the pastries, the children would gather round and want to eat them, because they did not usually have them. But HuiZhen said, 'These are for Dad and no one is allowed to eat them.' The children were very obedient; they did not ask for them, but just looked at them intently.

One day, Song TianZhen, the daughter of Dr John Sung, visited HuiZhen. She said to her, 'I'm Dr Sung's daughter. I met you during a prison visit. The Spirit prompted me to give you some Western pastries.' These Western pastries were very expensive in those days. Song TianZhen was really a very kind person. HuiZhen did not know her but had met her when she was in Beijing Prison visiting her sister Song TianYing. Song TianZhen told HuiZhen that she had seen the name Yuan in her father's diary for 1936. In that year, Yuan had been one of a few thousand participants who attended Dr Sung's second nationwide Bible exposition conference. HuiZhen was very touched by the fact that as a well-known speaker Dr Sung even took notice of the then young and insignificant Yuan. When HuiZhen took these pastries to Yuan and told him that they had been given by Song TianZhen, Yuan said, 'Dr John Sung passed away at a very young age. Many people did not understand why God did not give him a longer life so he could serve Him more. Now many of them have realised that it was actually the grace of God so that Dr Sung wouldn't have to suffer. If he were alive today, he would surely be in prison now.'

After he returned to Beijing Prison in 1962, he worked in the prison towel factory. Later, he was transferred to the plastics factory, where his job was to dye Chinese chess pieces. Yuan did all these indoor jobs quite well. In 1964, after his eldest daughter was married, his son-in-law told HuiZhen, 'Mum, I haven't met Dad yet. I'd like to meet him on next visiting day.' A month later, AnHu took her husband to visit Yuan. Yuan was delighted that his daughter had grown up and got married. It gave him a sense of achievement.

In the latter part of October 1965, his second son, FuSheng, applied to join the army in Ningxia and was accepted. He was assigned to the Production and Building Division. Before leaving Beijing, he visited his father in First Prison in Youanmen. He did not go during the visiting hours, and at first they turned him away. But he refused to go and said, 'I'm leaving for Ningxia to serve in the army very soon and I don't know when I'll be back. Could you please help me?' Eventually, permission was granted. Yuan was very surprised to see his son. FuSheng told him that he was going to Ningxia and that he had come to say goodbye to him. Yuan was very happy to see him before he went, and holding FuSheng's hands, he said, 'You're already eighteen, it's time to be independent. Take care when you're on your own at your posting. Remember to write home often. As for me, everything's been fine. Don't worry. It's good for you to go to a farming village. My gospel ministry was also in farming villages.' He continued, 'Do you still have faith in God?' FuSheng replied, 'Yes, I do.' Yuan asked, 'Do you still know how to sing hymns?' He replied, 'Yes, I do. I'm especially familiar with Psalm 23 and can recite it.' Yuan was comforted. During the half-hour visit, they held each other's hands and talked softly. Not long after FuSheng had gone to Ningxia, he received a letter from home telling him that Yuan was being sent back to the North-east. After their meeting in 1965, they did not meet each other again for fourteen years until the end of 1979 when Yuan was released.

The best thing that happened in Yuan's prison life from 1962 to 1966 was getting to know Liu Hao, with whom he developed a deep friendship. Liu Hao had been a secondary school teacher who had been transferred to a farming village in 1958 where he had witnessed what a mess the government had made of the local administration. Since the farmers did not dare to voice their grievances, as a conscientious intellectual he had voiced his dissent and had thus been deemed a counter-revolutionary. He had been arrested and sentenced to life imprisonment. Yuan and he were in the same cell and they became close friends. They first got to know each other when they were carrying out their corrective work order. Later they talked about the reasons why they had been arrested. Yuan told Liu Hao, 'I'm a Christian. I was arrested because I refused to join the Three-Self Movement. But I'm innocent.' From that time onwards, whenever the moment was right, Yuan would share the gospel with Liu Hao. After hearing what Yuan had to say, Liu Hao felt that the God in whom Yuan believed was the true God, but due to the circumstances he was too afraid to accept the gospel. But the two men understood each other.

Beijing Prison was octagonal in shape with a triangular space in between the cells. During festive seasons, the prisoners were allowed to have 'free activities for catharsis' in the triangular cubicles. They did not have such opportunities in the overcrowded cells and were not allowed to talk during the corrective work order. Therefore, the only time Yuan and Liu Hao could talk was in this triangular cubicle during festive seasons. It became the classroom for Liu Hao's spiritual training. Liu Hao had read politics and philosophy at university and was a sincere seeker after truth. To suit his intellectual approach to faith, Yuan began with the Gospel of John, explaining to him the true Word and the true meaning of faith and life. Yuan also told him that prayer was the spiritual breath of believers and that Christians were not lonely even in prison because they could always communicate with God.

In those days, the cult of 'Yiguandao' was causing a great deal of trouble in China and the government was arresting witch doctors and witches. Many people were confused between superstition and true faith. One day, a officer from the disciplinary core gave Yuan some books on breaking superstition and said, 'Read them carefully. They will straighten out your thinking.' Yuan glanced at them and said, 'My faith has nothing to do with these superstitions. I won't read them.' The other inmates were shocked by his words because none of them dared to resist the orders of the officer from the disciplinary core. They were afraid that he might get himself into trouble. But the officer said, 'Since you do not belong in the category of superstition, you must be a monk.' Yuan said, 'I'm not a Buddhist monk – if I'm a monk, I must be a Western monk.' The officer burst out laughing and did not ask any more questions. From then on, Yuan was known in Beijing Prison as 'Western monk'.

Yuan and Liu Hao could talk together about any subject. During the monthly visits, they were often together in the queue, and therefore they had met each other's family. Once, Liu Hao said sadly, 'Here we are in prison. I wonder how my family is coping. I've got an elderly mother and a daughter. You've got an elderly mother, a wife and six children. How are they managing to live?'

Yuan said, 'They trust the Lord. God is love. Our love is not merely in words, but also in deeds and truth. My wife is also a Christian. I believe she is able to manage the household.'

In the latter part of 1965, Beijing Prison became over-crowded again. It was China's most tumultuous period since the start of the Cultural Revolution. At that time, the Sino-Russian relationship had improved and the clouds of war had dissipated, so the government decided again to send those who were serving longer sentences to the North-east. Liu Hao and Yuan, both serving life imprisonment for anti-revolution, were sent to the North-east once again.

Chapter 16

The Fourteen-year Term in the Prison in the North-east

(The Summer of 1966–the Winter of 1979)

In March 1966, along with more than two thousand other prisoners, Yuan was sent back by train to Heilongjiang in the North-east, the region where he had been imprisoned for more than a year about six years before. This time their destination was the barren land of the Yin (literally meaning 'voice') River, which was situated in the Gannan District of Qiqihar City. Its original name was the Yin (literally meaning 'dark') River, so named because ghosts were said to appear in this land. After the liberation of China, the name was changed to Yin (voice) in order to break this superstition.

It was a virgin land. The prisoners slept on the grass the first night they were there and, as six years before, they then began the task of building a prison for themselves, making the bricks before they could lay them. Yuan had now become a skilled bricklayer. When they first arrived at Yin River, though it was March, the temperature was below −30°C. Sometimes there were sandstorms. Each of the prisoners only had about 200g of sorghum and a bowl of vegetable soup for each meal. They curled up in a tight ball against the extreme cold when they slept at night. When Liu Hao felt that he could no longer stand all the difficulties, Yuan would encourage him, 'Our sufferings are insignificant in comparison with the crucifixion of our Lord Jesus. That is true suffering. Take heart!' Yuan also gave some of his food to Liu Hao and said, 'I'm not a big eater, I've got enough. You've got to eat more.' Actually he did not have enough for himself but he just wanted to show kindness even in these severe difficulties. The farm for corrective work orders by the Yin River was new and the warders were more lenient towards the prisoners than in the other prisons. They were given sorghum and black potatoes to eat. Each of them was given cotton clothes (7kg in weight) and a white shirt once a year. Yuan adjusted to life in prison in the North-east within a short time.

In November 1966, the turmoil of the Cultural Revolution spread into the prison. Outside the prison, people were shouting, 'Down with..., down with...'. To tighten their control on the prisoners, the Penitentiary Department decided to send those serving longer terms, including Yuan, to Qiqihar Prison. Regulations in Qiqihar Prison were stricter than on the farm but the quality of life was much better – better food and lighter work. Yuan was assigned to work making screws. Although a new skill, it was much easier than ploughing the land on the farm.

Had he not been transferred to the North-east in 1966, he might have been tortured to death during the Cultural Revolution. This was another example of God's special provision for his protection. While the prison in the North-east was not totally spared from the effects of the Cultural Revolution, conditions were much better than in Beijing Prison and outside the prison. However, as a counter-revolutionary, Yuan was not totally spared.

In those days, there was a daily two-hour political broadcast in the prison, after which every prisoner was required to give a short speech. Their speeches were all taken down. In 1968, after listening to the broadcast, Yuan said, 'We haven't heard any news about Liu ShaoQi these last two days. Could it be a sign of internal struggle in the Communist Party?' He never thought that his casual words would be reported to the warder. The next day, the chief warder came and interrogated Yuan. Yuan admitted that he had made the remark. The chief warder said, 'This is a very serious problem. We've neglected your re-education. Now, let me ask you, do you still believe in your God?' Yuan said, 'Yes, I do.' The chief warder said angrily, 'I think you are revealing your counter-revolutionary thinking. Let me ask you again, do you still believe in your God?' Yuan answered firmly, 'Yes, I do.' The chief warder said, 'You recalcitrant counter-revolutionary! Your problem cannot be solved through attending political classes. You must be punished severely!' He ordered Yuan to be put into solitary confinement. He was required to sit with his legs folded for 'soul searching' all day long except when he had his meals and when he was sleeping.

Solitary confinement was a prison within the prison. Yuan was put into a cell that was less than two metres in length and width, with no window. Before he was confined here, his buttons and belt were all taken away to prevent him from committing suicide. He was under constant surveillance to make sure he was sitting in the required posture. The solitary confinement cell was also known as the 'one-metre room'. It was very dark and Yuan needed to turn on the light even in the daytime. He could stand up, but could not walk. Sometimes two people were put into this cell. Most of those who were confined here only stayed for a few days, but Yuan was imprisoned here for half a year. He had only two meals a day. The food was pushed in through a small opening in the cell door. A wet towel was passed in through the small opening in the morning for Yuan to clean his hands and face. He had to urinate and move his bowels in the cell using a potty. Due to the poor ventilation, the cell was always very smelly.

Yuan was confined in these terrible conditions for six months. There was no sunlight, no air, no water for a bath, no physical movement and no change of clothes. His whole body had already been infested with lice. All these tortures rendered him sickly and weak. His eyes could hardly see clearly. It was the sustaining power of God that saw him through these six months. After he was released from solitary confinement, he could not walk and needed to hold the wall to help him to stand. He was almost disabled. But after his release, he managed to recover quickly. In view of the poor nourishment in the prison, his recovery really was the work of God.

By the spring of 1969, Qiqihar Prison had also become overcrowded so the chief warder decided to build a new branch prison in the Zhaoyuan District in the Nenjiang region of Heilongjiang. It was named GeZhi Prison and was adjacent to Daqing which was well known by the public because of its mining machinery factory. Yuan, along with more than one thousand prisoners, was transferred to the new prison in this barren land. As in the past, during the initial stage of their transfer they stayed in tents pitched within a wired compound and they were allowed to move freely within this compound. Once the prison had been built they worked on the farm. The land was very barren and there were tombs everywhere, and these had to be dug up before seeds could be sown. Yuan was assigned to a group in charge of clearing the land of tombs, weeds and stones. Even though the labour was hard, the prisoners had more freedom than in the regular prisons.

Yuan met an old friend at GeZhi Prison – Wu MuJia. MuJia was one of the eleven representatives who had refused to join the Three-Self Movement. He had been brought up by foreign missionaries and, when he had grown up, had been sent to the HuaBei Theological Seminary in the Teng District of Shandong Province. He had taught in Baichengzi in the North-east and later ministered at a church in Ertiao, Beijing. He was arrested in 1955 because of his refusal to join the Three-Self Movement and was sentenced to fifteen years' imprisonment. Having been arrested for the same reason, one would have thought that the two men would be very close. Yuan bumped into MuJia when he was working on the farm. He was very excited to see an old friend. Not being in the same group, their paths had never crossed before. Wu MuJia was transplanting rice shoots with his head bowed, so he did not see Yuan. As the prisoners were not allowed to talk while they carried out their corrective work order Yuan had to think of an idea to get his attention without being discovered by others. He came up with the idea of singing a Christian song loudly. He sang, 'The Lord has not promised smooth sailing or a rosy life'. On hearing the song, MuJia lifted up his head and saw Yuan but he immediately bowed his head again. Yuan thought that MuJia would continue his song as he was walking towards him, but he did not. Yuan sang the line again, but MuJia did not respond. Yuan was puzzled. It was not easy meeting another Christian under those circumstances, let alone an old friend who had been arrested for the same reason and was going through the same persecution. He could not understand. They met a few times after that. When Yuan saw that there was nobody around, he talked to him about the Christian faith, but MuJia did not respond. Later he found out that MuJia had renounced his faith. Once when Yuan went to MuJia's group wanting to lend him his tool for repairing boots, he found out that he was very close to the warder. He was addressed as Teacher Wu. Yuan discovered that not all who shared his sufferings persevered to the end.

In 1973, about 450 prisoners from Gezhi Prison were sent to build a new prison in a paddy field fifteen kilometres away in Zhaoyuan District adjacent to Jilin Province, with the Nenjiang River as the boundary. Yuan and Liu Hao were among those sent. As Yuan was assigned to the group working in the paddy fields and Liu Hao to the group working in the plantation, they had less opportunity to talk to each other.

The chief warder had been in the army and was not very well educated. He regarded Christians as agents of the USA. However, due to Yuan's excellent performance and diligence in carrying out the corrective work order, he treated him well. The soldiers hated slaughtering chickens, so Yuan did the job for them. The chief warder wanted to release Yuan early, so he gave him some newspaper clippings arguing against superstition, hoping that he would recant his faith. But Yuan insisted that he was different from the others, and that he was a Western monk. The chief warder laughed at that and did not press him further. Yuan was very hard-working, and was very thrifty in his use of materials and resources. He always volunteered to take notes at meetings. His one drawback was that he could not work as fast as others and, however hard he tried, he could only harvest 20 per cent of the amount others achieved. Hard work was another way in which prisoners could reduce their prison terms – in addition to making accusations against fellow prisoners, which Yuan refused to do – and because of this, Yuan failed to reduce his term. Since he had received his sentence of life imprisonment, he had not thought about being released.

Another problem for Yuan was his short-sightedness, which affected his work on the farm. In addition to his inexperience in agricultural work, he was always slower, especially when he was weeding, and he could hardly distinguish between grass and paddy, so he often weeded out rice together with weeds. In the spring of 1977, after he had weeded some rice along with grass, the supervisor noticed and got very angry. 'Whose work is this?' he roared. 'The rice was weeded out along with the grass!' The supervisor reported this to the warder and Yuan was accused of sabotage. He was punished in a 'reprimand meeting' where he was pushed onto the stage and 'reprimanded' by everyone. The prisoners shouted at him, and some of them went up on the stage, and made all sorts of false accusations (for the reduction of their own sentence); some even beat him. Liu Hao could stand it no longer. He went to the warder and said, 'We who are from Beijing can hardly distinguish between grass and rice. Sometimes, I also make mistakes. I don't believe that Yuan did it on purpose. He is inexperienced, and that is why he makes mistakes.' The warder was furious and accused Liu Hao of covering up the sabotage of a counter-revolutionary and ordered him to do 'soul-searching'.

Meanwhile, Yuan remained very calm on the 'reprimanding' stage. It seemed as if he was indifferent to what was happening to him. After the incident, Liu Hao asked him about what he had been feeling. Yuan said, 'Without God's permission, I will not lose even one hair. I'm not bothered at all by how I'm treated. To me they are a bunch of lunatics. Let them scream and shout. I'm relying on my Lord and I won't be crushed by external pressures.'

As a result Yuan was again put under close surveillance as a punishment for his 'disobedience'. His freedom was curtailed and he was not allowed to talk and move around freely. Basically, his freedom was denied, although not as severely as in solitary confinement. In order to punish him further, they assigned him to do the dirtiest and heaviest work, such as cleaning the toilets, and he was also given less and poorer food than his fellow inmates.

Just as this period of close surveillance was coming to an end, FuLe, his fourth son, visited him while on a business trip to the North-east. When Yuan had been arrested in 1958, FuLe had been eleven years old and had been in primary school. He had done very well academically but, because of the financial constraints, worked in a petroleum gas factory in Chishui, Guizhou. On his business trip he stopped en route in Beijing to see his mother and discussed with her his plan to visit his father. He had not met his father for eleven years. HuiZhen bought a lot of canned food, pastries and sweets for him to take to his father. So FuLe set out to the North-east with all this food.

After a whole night's journey by train, he arrived first at Harbin interchange where he took a train headed towards Taikang. Then he intended to take a taxi to Gezhi Prison. The temperature in Harbin City was −29°C. He had to fight his way through a slight sandstorm caused by the icy-cold north wind. When he found the taxi stand, he discovered that there was only one trip to Gezhi daily, and that was at 6.00 a.m. so he would have to wait until the next day. He put up at a hostel for the night. The hostel was a lodging place for those who pulled handcarts and there were more than ten people sleeping there. It was so dirty that the white blankets had turned grey; he could only tell that they had once been white because of the folds in the material. He said to himself, 'Well, it doesn't matter. I'm leaving tomorrow. At least this place is near the taxi stand.' No sooner had he lain down than he began to feel hungry. He suddenly realised that he had not eaten any dinner but, as there was no canteen or food stall in the hostel, he had to put up with the hunger. He had some pastries brought from Beijing in his bag, but he did not want to eat the food intended for his father. Having slept for a few hours, he left the hostel and arrived at the taxi stand at 5.00 a.m. He saw a noodle shop that had opened for business by the taxi stand. It only opened when there was a trip. FuLe ate a bowl of noodles and then took a taxi at 6.00 a.m., arriving at Gezhi at 8.00 a.m. Seeing the barren land near the prison, he felt a surge of emotion when he thought of his father having to endure all this. He asked a passer-by for directions to the prison and was told it was three kilometres away and, as there was no taxi, he had to walk. This was not an easy task for FuLe with all his luggage but, thank God, at least the weather was much better than the day before. There was no wind at all, so it was much warmer. He strode happily, knowing that he would see his father in a very short while. After walking for an hour, he arrived at Gezhi Prison. FuLe liaised with the chief warder and was granted permission to see his father after he had produced some documents to prove that he was on a business trip.

After he had waited about ten minutes, FuLe saw his father come and bow to the warder. The warder said, 'Yuan, guess who has come to visit you.' Yuan lifted up his head but, when he saw the lanky young man before him, he could not recognise that this was his son. He asked, 'Who are you?' FuLe said, 'Dad, it is I. I'm FuLe.' Yuan felt a sudden surge of strong emotions when he finally recognised his son. Tears streamed down his face. The warder said, 'Your son has come to visit you. You should be glad. Don't be so sad.' There were also tears in FuLe's eyes. He could still recognise his father, but he had aged. They had not met each other for more than ten years. Since Yuan's transfer away from Beijing in 1966, he had missed his father. Though he looked much older now, he was still in good spirits.

The warder ordered Yuan to take a seat and beckoned FuLe to a seat two metres away from him. They were both speechless for a moment. At that time, Yuan was still under close surveillance. The warder said, 'Yuan, your son has come all this way to visit you. You must tell him how you have been corrected. Tell him how you were put into solitary confinement because of your recalcitrant counter-revolutionary stance. Tell him also how you sabotaged the work by weeding out the rice along with grass. You must pull your socks up from now on. Most of those who were imprisoned at the same time as you have had their term reduced. You are one of the few who is still recalcitrant after almost twenty years of imprisonment. From now onwards you must lean more towards the Communist Party and its leaders. Don't resist, otherwise there'll be no hope for you.' When FuLe heard this, he thought, 'My father's eye-sight is very weak, and he is inexperienced in farm work. Could he distinguish between grass and rice?' Yuan looked at FuLe, and asked, 'How are the rest of the family?' So FuLe updated him about what had happened in the family recently. He told his father not to worry about his mother because she was coping well. Yuan nodded and reminded him to wear more clothes when he was in the North-east. After about forty minutes, FuLe suddenly remembered the food he had brought. When he was giving the food to his father, the warder said it was too much – only a small portion was allowed. FuLe pleaded with the warder, 'I've come from so far away, please allow me to give this food to my father.' But his request was denied.

When Yuan was led away by two warders, he bowed his head in despair. He avoided eye-contact with FuLe fearing that he might not be able to hold back his tears. His son did the same, fearing that he too would be overcome with emotion. After he had left the prison, FuLe continued his business trip. As soon as he had arrived at Harbin, he sent a telegram to his mother, saying, 'I've visited Dad. Everything is fine. Don't worry. I'll tell you the details when I come home.' He knew that his mother would be having sleepless nights thinking about the trip.

During the twenty-one years and eight months of his imprisonment, Yuan spent sixteen years in the North-east. When he had been arrested, he had been relatively young and not all that strong physically. When he had been sentenced to life imprisonment, many had thought that he would not survive the poor conditions of prison life. When he was transferred to the North-east, Yuan had thought that he would die there. But against all the odds, God saw him through these years and trained him for His greater use. God not only protected his life but also granted him good health. Usually, the hard labour of the corrective work order would lead to one of three consequences:

1. loss of sanity,
2. suicide, or
3. improvement of health through physical exertion.

Yuan fell into the third category. In the cold North-east, he had to work for at least nine hours a day. Despite the extreme conditions, Yuan had not fallen ill except for catching a minor cold once. During the twenty-one years of prison life God had taught him many things. His experience in the North-east was indeed God's grace to him. Having to carry soil on a shoulder pole as part of his work, he would often fall in the icy and snowy fields. He learnt to straighten his back, for it was easier to fall when his back was curved. Through such training, even into his eighties Yuan had not developed a hunchback. Years of a vegetarian diet also cured his digestive problems. He had been to many fields of corrective work order in the North-east, some of whose names he had forgotten. He had never imagined that he would come back alive and continue to serve the Lord for a few decades after his return.

Even though he could not explain his sufferings, he never doubted the faithfulness and love of God. He believed that whatever he endured originated from God for his good. He submitted to the sovereignty of God and had never hated the Communist Party. That was the reason that he could labour and learn happily throughout his imprisonment. It was the miraculous work of God that preserved his life and saw him through these tough years.

During his years in prison he had no access to the Bible. He meditated on the scripture verses that he had memorised in the past. Sometimes, he wrote these verses down and showed them to Liu Hao in secret. During his imprisonment, two hymns, 'Psalm 27' and 'The Old Rugged Cross', continually inspired and encouraged him. During the rest periods of his daily labour, when other inmates were drinking water and smoking, he would sing these two hymns. He was empowered by their message: 'I want to lift up my voice in praise of His glorious cross until I appear before His judgement seat and hear him saying to me, "My good and faithful servant. Exchange your cross for a crown."'

God requires faithfulness. Yuan kept asking himself, 'Are you faithful to what the Lord has entrusted to you?' The icy-cold wind of the North-east had been a witness many times to the prayer of God's servant, 'O Lord, I could have enjoyed a more comfortable life had I gone astray from You. But I remember how my Lord Jesus Christ was obedient unto death. May I be Your faithful servant. I'm willing to be faithful to the end.'

PART VI

'A prudent wife is from the Lord'

Chapter 17

The Family Background and Conversion of Liang HuiZhen

Liang HuiZhen was born in 1919 in Zhaoqing, Guangdong. She was five years younger than Yuan. Both her mother and grandmother were Buddhists. Her grandfather, Liang YaoNan, who had graduated from the Guangdong Naval Academy, had participated in the Sino-Japanese War during the Ching Dynasty (1894–5). Having used English in his work, he had a good command of the language. He was later assigned to work at the Tianjin Railway Department. The family lived in a bungalow and was comfortably off.

HuiZhen's father, Liang ChenJi, was a graduate of the Nankai University. Her mother, Lin GuiHao, was the daughter of a capitalist; the family hired maids who cooked and tailored. HuiZhen received a Western education, attending kindergarten at age five and beginning her primary education at age six at the Railway Primary School. Six years later, she went up to Bethel Secondary School before transferring, in her junior middle three year, to a missionary school, Yangshan Secondary School. In those days it was fashionable to send children to missionary schools, principally because they provided a formal English education. Although HuiZhen did not believe in Jesus at that time, while she was at Yangshan Secondary School an AOG teacher left a deep impression on her. When his wife fell ill, he did not take her to see a doctor, but laid his hands on her and prayed for her loudly. She had to take Bible lessons at school and was required to memorise Scripture verses. As a keen participator in the performing arts, HuiZhen acted in many gospel dramas. After she graduated from senior middle school, she went up to the renowned Sanba[1] Girls School, which had been set up by the Teachers' College for Women.

HuiZhen's family and Yuan's family came from the same village and Yuan's maternal grandmother and HuiZhen's paternal grandmother were foster sisters. The two families were very close. Yuan's mother and grandmother often visited the Liangs. During the 7 July Lugou Bridge incident, when the Japanese troops bombarded Tianjin, HuiZhen and the other eight members of her family narrowly escaped from a bomb. Fortunately, none of her family members were hurt. Her mother only managed to salvage a little money; the rest was looted by the Japanese troops. HuiZhen saw first hand the cruelty of war when she witnessed six bombs being dropped by a fighter jet. As the bombs exploded on the ground and buildings burst into flames there were people running everywhere, crying and screaming; some were injured, some were killed. HuiZhen was terrified. She suddenly thought of Jesus and knew that it was only He who could save her. In the horror of that situation, she said the first prayer of her life, 'O Lord, save me. Life is horrible.' After the bombardment, it started raining and was very cold. Sitting helplessly by the road, their clothes soaked through and completely chilled, and seeing so many refugees passing by, HuiZhen came to terms with the harsh realities of life for the first time: life was so fragile. There was only a thin line between life and death. Trembling in fear, HuiZhen knew that she needed God. She kept crying out to God, 'O Lord, I need You. Save me.' From 7.00 a.m. until that night, they sat by the roadside. There were corpses everywhere. In the afternoon, the refugees sought asylum in the Italian concession. In those days the city had designated areas called 'concessions' and these were not bombed. Japan, Great Britain, France and Italy all had concessions. However, the Italians not only denied the refugees entry to their concession, but they also sprayed them with water and chased them away. A few hours later, a man waving a flag shouted to the refugees to come to a refugee camp which had been established, and they ran to safety. Some hawkers who sold biscuits took advantage of the situation by raising the price of a biscuit to one dollar, but, having not eaten for a whole day, the refugees fought over the biscuits. HuiZhen's family only managed to buy two biscuits for them all. Later, they were given free porridge. They stayed in the refugee camp for three days, sleeping on mats as there were no beds. Three days later, through a friend, her father managed to rent a house for fifteen dollars in the French concession. But her mother missed the bungalow in Hebeixindalu, Tianjin. They decided to move back after the situation stabilised. Since young women were in great danger from the Japanese soldiers, HuiZhen's parents left her and her younger sister, also now a young adult, in the concession when they and the other children moved back.

The war had completely changed HuiZhen's life. Through it, she had come to know the Lord.

The end of man is the beginning of God. In those fearful days, HuiZhen began to read the Bible seriously. She also began to learn to cook. After the war, Yuan went to visit HuiZhen and her family in Tianjin. He shared the gospel with HuiZhen's mother, but she was not interested. At that time HuiZhen was still living in the concession, so they did not meet. In September 1937, HuiZhen went to stay at Yuan's house for two nights when she took an entrance examination at one of the schools in Beijing. Yuan shared the gospel with her and she responded positively, but due to the briefness of the visit they did not talk further. She passed the entrance examination but, when she became a Christian, she changed her mind and withdrew from the school, having decided she wanted to study theology. Her withdrawal disappointed her family members, especially her grandmother who had been saving up for her college fees. In September, while HuiZhen was still living in the concession, she contacted Mr Pan ZiFeng, the Principal of the Tianjin Bible College, which had been recommended by Yuan. It belonged to the same denomination as Yuan's seminary, the

Holiness Movement. Eventually, however, because the college did not provide accommodation and her parents were worried about her safety, she did not enrol. HuiZhen made up by reading Christian literature, having her own personal devotions and attending Christian meetings. From 1937 to 1938 she attended the Holy Tabernacle Church led by Zhang ZhouXin in Yaohua in the French concession, where she was baptised in May 1938. In the early part of 1938, Yuan completed his field education there.

Seeing HuiZhen's commitment to attending Christian meetings after she was converted, her mother was worried for her safety. However, when she saw the changes in her daughter, especially in her temper, she was very glad. Although she had not yet believed, she knew that, to make such a change in a person's life, Jesus must be a powerful person.

One day, HuiZhen saw a letter in her father's study with the return address of Yuan's family in Beijing on it, and opened it. The letter, in extremely elegant handwriting, was written in a mixture of classical and modern Chinese. It was written by Yuan's father and proposed the marriage of HuiZhen and Yuan. Because her parents were unhappy about Yuan's family background, they were hesitant and had not discussed it with her. After she had read the letter, she felt a surge of shyness but she could not stop thinking about it. After a few days, she wondered why her parents had not brought the subject up. She felt torn apart thinking about it. On the one hand, Yuan was not good looking, but on the other she was glad that he was a pastor as she had been looking for a believing husband.

One Saturday, when her father was on leave, HuiZhen's parents asked her to come and talk with them in the sitting room. He said, 'HuiZhen, we've got something to discuss with you. Yuan's father has written from Beijing proposing that you and Yuan marry. Your mother and I have discussed it but I don't think we can agree. Why don't you think this over for a week and decide for yourself?'

HuiZhen nodded. She began to pray about her marriage and, after a period of prayer, she realised that wealth and looks were not important criteria for a life partner; the most important criterion was her future husband's character. She knew that Yuan loved the Lord and had put his life on the line for his faith. For this reason she decided to accept his proposal but she still had doubts. She knew that life with Yuan would be difficult financially, and she was afraid. However, in the end the knowledge of his love for the Lord prevailed. She asked for a sign from the Lord: 'O Lord, if it is Your will, give me peace of mind. I don't care if he is rich or good looking. What I ask is that he should love You, and that we can serve You together in the future.' After this God gave her the inner peace she desired. On Sunday, when her father brought up the proposal, she said that she wanted to accept. After much thought, her father said, 'You're still very young. I must warn you that though he's a good man, he's too poor. I'm afraid he won't even be able to support the family when you have children. You may live to regret it. Think about your future; otherwise you'll suffer.' HuiZhen said, 'The most important thing in my life is to rely on the Lord.' On hearing this, her parents looked at each other. Her father tried again to dissuade her, 'You'd better think very carefully. Don't rush into this decision.' HuiZhen said emphatically, 'I've made up my mind.' Then her father said, 'Since you've made up your mind, we've won't say anything more. But, when you face difficulties in the future, especially when you have children, don't regret it. We've introduced so many good men to you, but you didn't want them: you want him. So don't blame us later if you have regrets.' He sent a letter to Yuan's father, accepting the proposal.

In May 1938, Yuan and HuiZhen were officially engaged in Tianjin and got married on 22 July in Beijing. When it came to the wedding arrangements, HuiZhen's mother said, 'We've got a lot of children, but since HuiZhen is our eldest daughter, her wedding cannot be taken lightly. We'll give her a dowry.' Even though Yuan said that Christians didn't need one, she insisted. She tailored a wedding costume for Yuan and gave HuiZhen four boxes of new clothes. She also wanted to give Yuan a new set of furniture but he refused, saying, 'We Christians don't need all this. After all, Tianjin is

not our home. As a pastor, I don't have a permanent home.'
So HuiZhen's mother gave him 700 silver dollars. After their
marriage, whenever they were in financial crisis, they would
dip into this dowry.

Even though HuiZhen had heard about the Christian faith
in the missionary school and had accepted the gospel during
the incident on 7 July, her spiritual growth was very much
due to Yuan. After their marriage, HuiZhen became her
husband's best helper and closest spiritual partner. They
studied the Bible, sang hymns, prayed and served the Lord
together, and together they endured much suffering. But
they also tasted the goodness of the Lord. Everyone who
knew HuiZhen appreciated that she was a very intelligent
and able woman, very sharp thinking and skilled in working
with her hands. Her educational background enabled her to
study God's Word in depth and her endurance saw her
through many difficulties.

At the beginning of their married life, HuiZhen could
hardly do any of the chores around the house. On the third
day after their wedding, in order to reduce their expenses,
Yuan's mother laid off their maid and HuiZhen had to learn
how to do the chores. She brought up the six children all on
her own. She often carried her child in one arm and washed
the clothes with the other hand. Yuan had a very quick
temper. When he was studying the Bible, he would spread his
books all over the table and not tidy the mess afterwards up,
so HuiZhen would tidy up for him. But afterwards, if he could
not find a book, he would get mad at her and HuiZhen would
have to bear with him. Whenever he wanted anything she
would see to it straightaway. She honoured her husband very
much and wholeheartedly supported his ministry.

When their eldest son, FuYin, began to walk, HuiZhen
would take him with her and accompany Yuan to spread the
gospel in Dongguan, Cheng'an District, Hebei. Apart from
taking care of the family, she also taught as a volunteer
teacher. It was a difficult life. In 1942, when the Japanese
launched a surprise attack on Pearl Harbour and Yuan was
out of town, HuiZhen hid in the cellar while the Japanese
took over the church and looted all of their clothes.

Their life in the Shanhu village in Cheng'an District was completely different from the easy life that she had enjoyed before her marriage. Their second child, AnHu, was born prematurely at seven months while Yuan was out spreading the gospel in the villages. The delivery was difficult and HuiZhen almost lost her life. The premature birth was due to inadequate prenatal care but HuiZhen thought that it was related to an incident when she was drying the bedsheets and stood on tiptoes to look over the clothesline.

The living conditions in the village at that time were very poor. They could not afford a maid and, three days after she delivered AnHu, when Yuan went out to lead meetings, she had to work on the farm. Their diet consisted of pickles, *wowotou* and millet porridge. In addition to breast-feeding, HuiZhen had to milk goats for extra milk for AnHu. She had to pick sorghum leaves to make a fire and feed the goats, and she also had to collect cotton. In order to be able to have light, she had to extract oil from flowers for the lamp. In the village she had to do all kinds of work. One day, she had to work quite a distance from the house, so she put AnHu to sleep in a mosquito net. When she came home, she discovered that AnHu had fallen out of the mosquito net into the mud. She had cried herself to sleep in the mud and, as the tears and urine wet the soil, her body was covered with mud. HuiZhen was very distressed by this experience and wept as she bathed AnHu four times. Sometimes, when she was free, she had to teach the old women hymns, and read the Bible to them. They only ate buns during festive seasons. But HuiZhen never complained about this difficult life. Yuan said to her, 'I never thought that as a lady from a rich family, you would be willing to eat *wowotou* and live in a shack with me.' HuiZhen said, 'I don't mind any of these things.' God moulded her through her experiences in the village. She went through a lot of difficulties, but she never regretted her choice. Once when Yuan went to town, he bought a loaf of bread for HuiZhen, knowing that she had not eaten bread for a long while. She was very thankful for the thought, but felt that it was too wasteful, so they pushed the bread back and forwards between each other, and neither of them was willing to eat it.

Having taken care of her father-in-law in the final weeks of his life, fulfilling Yuan's filial duties on his behalf when he had to return to the village to continue his ministry, HuiZhen also cared for her mother-in-law every day when she was seriously ill. As she needed to eat some nutritious food such as *duzhongzI*[2] and pig kidney every day, HuiZhen got up very early in the morning to buy them in the market. Through persistent prayer, her mother-in-law recovered gradually until finally she was able to be up and about. Because of God's healing power in her life, she turned from her resistance of God to fear of God and began to share the gospel with everyone she met.

In order to be able to concentrate on his ministry Yuan seldom concerned himself with household matters but delegated them all to HuiZhen. However, he took particular interest in the education of their children, especially in their religious education and organising them to do their household chores. Some of the children were assigned to fetch church members, some to make fires, some to clean the sanctuary and some to distribute hymnbooks. Due to Yuan's busyness in his work and his tendency to take things a bit too seriously, he seldom took his children out to play and did not know how to communicate with them. As a result, they were afraid of him. HuiZhen acted as a kind of buffer in the family. Her cheerful disposition brought warmth to the family while her intelligence and skilfulness brought order. She was a very detailed and meticulous person and was always a good example to the family. Together Yuan and HuiZhen provided a warm family environment.

She knew what it was to be in need, and she knew what it was to have plenty. Through Christ who strengthened her, she could overcome everything. When she went home after four years in the countryside, her mother wept when she saw how dark and skinny she had become. Her mother wanted her to stay with her longer so that she could feed her up with some nutritious food, but she could not stay long, for she had to return to Beijing to serve the Lord alongside Yuan.

In 1946, after the launching of the Gospel Hall in Beijing, their primary income was from Yuan's work as a translator. The rest of their income came from the collection of offerings from the congregation, but as the congregation was small, the collection was very limited. However difficult their financial situation was, she would still open her house to visitors, especially the blind, and would always treat them to meals whenever they called in. She always said that God's grace was more than sufficient. Through her experience of difficulties she came to know the Lord deeper and trusted him more.

HuiZhen said that Yuan had very obvious strengths and weakness. As a man with backbone his strengths included holding firmly to truth, integrity, abstention from gossip, honesty, undivided attention to work and loyalty to the Lord. His weakness was his bad temper. But throughout their sixty years of marriage they never fought (physically) and as far as HuiZhen could remember they only quarrelled once. On that occasion, she had bought a box of pastries for Yuan to take to Tianjin for his mother. Yuan was unhappy about this, because he did not think that Christians should concern themselves with such matters. He cancelled his trip and ate the pastries himself. Because of his unfortunate early experience of family life, family relationships were not high on his list of priorities. This lack of sensitivity was one of the reasons why he could survive the emotional turmoil in the prison. He was skilled in personal evangelism, and was very hardworking, although not very tactful. HuiZhen's sensitivity and wisdom complemented him. Throughout the years, Yuan did not remember her birthday, but she never complained. She knew that, whenhe was engrossed in his ministry of spreading the gospel, he would leave the whole world behind him. Actually, he could not even remember his own birthday. He only knew that it was in the sixth month of the lunar calendar. Yuan recognised that HuiZhen had been a great help to him and always said that 80 per cent of his ministry was dependent on her. She always said that this was too much of an exaggeration.

Notes

1. Literally means three and eight or thirty-eight.
2. [Chinese medicine] the bark of eucommia (*Eucommia ulmoides*).

Chapter 18

The Plight of Yuan's Family During His Imprisonment

From April 1958, when Yuan was arrested, for more than twenty years HuiZhen had to take care of her elderly mother-in-law and her children. As a housewife, how could she support the family? Though she had mentally prepared for the arrest of her husband, she was still devastated when it happened.

Before his arrest, Yuan did not receive any salary from any organisation. They served the Lord by faith. As a result, they did not have any savings and, after his arrest, the Gospel Hall had to close down. The family was soon in a desperate financial situation and HuiZhen went through the most difficult six months of her life, with the constant worry about how they would survive. All they could afford to eat was porridge, but porridge could not supply the nutritional needs of growing children and an aging mother-in-law. When they did not have enough porridge for everyone, HuiZhen would go without. In the face of such difficulties, she became very distressed and began to question God, 'Oh Lord, my husband was imprisoned for Your sake. Now I've got to take care of both the old and the young in the family, but I'm unemployed. How shall I carry this heavy load?'

The financial difficulties were not the only cause of her depression. In addition, she felt abandoned when some believers began to keep their distance from her family after Yuan's arrest. People who had received help from her family avoided her and pretended that they had not seen her when they met in the street. Some of them did not dare to enter her house because they were afraid of being followed. A lady, whose father was a pastor and who used to be very committed to serving the Lord by copying the Bible for Wang MingDao, later deserted the House Church Movement and joined the Three-Self Movement. Wang MingDao was very angry when he found out. Yuan had also advised her not to join the Three-Self Movement. After Yuan's arrest, she even denied knowing him. She said that she'd only heard of him. Not until forty years later, in 1998, did she acknowledge that she did know him. At that time she was asked the question again and she said, 'Yes, I do. But he fell out with me when I joined the Three-Self Movement.' Questions were posed, and differing answers received. This shows how varying political situations can affect a person's psychology.

When Yuan was arrested, his eldest child was seventeen while the youngest was six years old. All of them were still in school. In order to put up a good front, HuiZhen did not allow herself to betray her sadness in front of her children but she often wept secretly. The older children understood what their mother was feeling, so they did not mention their father. But the youngest daughter was still very innocent and kept asking, 'Where's Dad? Why is he not home yet?' HuiZhen would tell her, 'Your Dad has gone to political classes. He'll be back after the classes.' When she did not see her father after waiting for a long time, she asked again, 'Isn't Dad coming back? Doesn't Dad want to see me any more?' And then she would cry. One day, after playing in the courtyard with her friends for a short while, she came back in tears and told her mother that the other children had bullied her and laughed at her, saying that she had no father, and had refused to play with her. She asked, 'Is Dad still alive?' HuiZhen said, 'Yes, he is still alive. Don't listen to their nonsense. If they don't want to play with you, let them be.' As she consoled her daughter, she too could feel the pain.

After Yuan's arrest, the Gospel Hall in Beijing was taken back by the landlord and the family moved to a room in the White Pagoda Temple. After the police had searched the house, all the family was left with was a few bundles of belongings. During the great revolution, the bronze bed that Yuan and she had bought for their wedding had been seized to be smelted for steel. So HuiZhen spread out some bricks on the floor and put planks on top of them, and the whole family slept on that as their bed. A water tank and a few boxes were all they had.

During the first three months after Yuan's arrest, HuiZhen did not have any income, so she had to sell what belongings she had left. The anguish she felt and the despair plunged her into a deep depression. She had never in her life experienced anything like it. She went down on her knees and prayed to the Lord every night. But these were not prayers of trust, but prayers of struggle – struggles with God. She kept arguing with God, and asking, 'Why would You allow all this to happen to me? Why won't You listen to my prayer and rescue me from my troubles?' The more she argued with God, the more burdened she felt; the more burdened she felt, the more she argued with God. She was trapped in a vicious cycle. But the Lord remained silent. Eventually, she was overwhelmed by her heavy burden.

In her most desperate moment, when God seemed not to have listened to her prayer, the word of God came to her, 'All these are from Me.'

'Oh no, Lord, You would not cause us all these sufferings!'

'All these are from Me! For My will is higher than your will, and My way is higher than your way.'

At that moment, HuiZhen was comforted and strengthened. She surrendered once again before the Lord and prayed to Him, 'Since these are from You, I'll speak no more. My only request is that You will protect me and each of my family members so that we will not dishonour Your name whatever circumstances we face.'

After that, her heavy load disappeared. She prayed, 'O Lord, I believe that You'll sustain me and see me through all my difficulties. I'll carry my cross and follow You forever.'

At that time, with no income, all the food at home was soon gone. Her mother-in-law, staring at the rice container which was almost empty, said, 'Tomorrow let's go to my daughter's house.' On hearing this, HuiZhen was very upset, but she was not willing to let her mother-in-law starve along with them. So she prayed to God. God comforted her with His Word,

> *'Look at the birds of the air; they do not sow or reap or store away in barns, and yet your heavenly Father feeds them. Are you not much more valuable than they?'*   (Matthew 6:26)

The next morning someone knocked at the door. When HuiZhen opened the door, she saw an old woman who was a stranger to her. She looked at HuiZhen and asked, 'Is this the house of the Yuans?' She said it was. She asked again, 'Is this the house of Brother Yuan?' HuiZhen assumed that she must be a Christian because very few people who weren't Christians dared to call on the home of a prisoner, so she invited her in and asked her, 'How should I address you?' The old woman smiled and said, 'I've been looking for you ever since you moved house. For the past few days, the Holy Spirit has been urging me to come to this place.' As she spoke, she handed an envelope and a small wallet to HuiZhen.

The old woman did not identify herself. After she had left, HuiZhen opened the wallet and found in it fifty dollars. In those days, fifty dollars were equivalent to the food expenses of her whole family for two months. HuiZhen could not hold back her tears of thanksgiving. She said, 'O Lord, You're truly a faithful God. You make no mistakes. What a woman of little faith I am.'

Five months after Yuan's arrest, HuiZhen found a job on a construction site, but she was poorly paid, only receiving a daily wage of eighty cents. She only earned twenty-four dollars even if she worked every day of the month. Her salary could hardly support the expenses of a large family and the tuition fees of her children. The children were very sensitive to the family's financial situation. They began to walk to school and took turns paying their tuition fees.

God moved many unknown believers to supply their needs. An old Christian woman from the North-east who was known as Yidaniang sent a piece of frozen meat in a can to HuiZhen. In those days, meat was rationed. Yidaniang exchanged the ration tickets that she had saved for half a year for this piece of meat. She sent a message to HuiZhen along with the meat, 'I don't mind eating less meat. You've got to take care of six children and a mother-in-law. This is for you.' Many of the believers who sent money to HuiZhen sent it from fake addresses, and so most of her thank-you cards were sent back to her. HuiZhen gave all the thanks to the Lord. Once she received a postal order sent from No. 20 Emmaus Road. HuiZhen could not reply to the sender for there was no such road in Beijing.

HuiZhen did not tell her family about Yuan's arrest because many of them did not believe in Jesus and she was afraid that the news would drive them further away from the Lord. After almost one year, her brother came to visit her when he was in Beijing on business. When he did not see Yuan, he asked, 'Where is brother-in-law?' HuiZhen tried to change the subject. After he had asked three times, HuiZhen finally gave in. She said, 'OK, let me tell you what has happened. He has been in prison for almost a year. I've been keeping it secret because I was afraid that you might be over-anxious for me. Please don't tell Mum. I'm afraid she could not take it.' Her brother said, 'You should have told me earlier. How can you endure all these sufferings alone? I'm not afraid of being implicated. We're brother and sister. Now that you're in such a difficult situation, I should help you.' As he spoke, he took out some money, handed it to her and said, 'Take this money for cloth and make some clothes for the children. Now that brother-in-law is not around, it's my obligation to take care of you.' After that, he sent money to HuiZhen once a month. From then on, other members of her family began to find out that Yuan had been arrested. Her mother sent some clothes and food to her. During Chinese New Year, HuiZhen would take all the children back to her mother's for four days. She went home every Chinese New Year until her mother passed away in 1974.

However difficult life was, HuiZhen did not neglect her children's education. God graciously preserved these six children so that none of them was unruly. She always prayed for her children, 'O God, may none of my family dishonour Your name.' She always said, 'My children are brought up by God. In such circumstances, it would be very easy for them to go off the rails but they are all very obedient'. A man once said, 'Look at how obedient Yuan's six children are. They never quarrel. This is indeed the grace of God. You can sense the presence of God through his children.' All of them learnt how to cook at a very young age. After school they did not go off to play, but rushed home to help with the cooking. When one of their teachers found out, she said to HuiZhen, 'It is indeed an enormous task for you to bring up these six children as a single parent. And it's incredible that you are doing so well.' HuiZhen said, 'We're Christians. We are bringing up our children according to the Word of God.'

Six months after his father's arrest, FuYin dropped out of school and enrolled in Shougang Vocational School. He made this decision so that he could graduate and work as soon as possible so as to support the family. While he was studying at the vocational school, he worked part time and earned a monthly salary of sixteen dollars. He would give ten dollars to his mother and keep the rest for his expenses. FuLe, the fourth child, studied in Fuchengmen, Beijing and did very well at school. He was one of the top thirty-five students in Zhongdian Secondary School. In those days, schools were in as much uproar as society, and most of the students could not concentrate on their studies. FuLe, however, studied hard and often scored top marks. Due to their financial situation, he could not afford bus fares so he walked to school every day and he brought food from home for his lunch. He ate leftover *wowotou* almost every day. At lunch-time, his classmates would jeer at him; they gave him the nickname: '*wowotou* brain'. But he was the first in the class in almost every examination. Some jealous classmates hurled insults at him, 'You *wowotou* brain. How can you do so well in your exams? Anyway, however well you do, you still have to eat *wowotou* every day.' FuLe was deeply hurt. He pleaded with his mother, 'Mum, why don't we eat buns? Can you give me a bun, just to silent my nasty classmates. Just this once, please?' HuiZhen was very upset but she said, 'No. We can only eat buns on the 1 June festival.'

Xiaoliu, the youngest daughter, did not have any woollen clothes until 1965. When her eldest sister, AnHu, got married she gave XiaoLiu her old woollen clothes. The family's life improved when AnHu got married. XiaoLiu was the head prefect in her primary school and was a committee member of the school's society. She was a well-rounded student, who did brilliantly well in every subject. Although she did very little school work at home, she was always the first in the class. She did not have a clear memory of her father and was not sure why he had been arrested. All she knew was that there was some kind of problem with her family which meant she had to work extra hard for acceptance, and even then it was no use. She was not allowed to participate in communal activities because her family was associated with a counter-revolutionary. In 1967, she changed her name to Liang YongHong, in an attempt to dissociate herself from her father, naively thinking that this would mean she would be accepted by society. In 1969, when she graduated from her junior middle high school, the school sent her to work in the countryside, even though that was not the norm. The registrar said, 'If it is not the counter-revolutionaries who should be sent to the countryside, who should it be?' XiaoLiu realised that she would never be accepted by this unfair society. When Yuan found all this out after his release, he did not blame her for he understood the pressures she had to face as a young girl.

Three days after HuiZhen had started work on the construction site as a construction worker, the supervisor discovered that she was a well-educated woman, and had good handwriting and was very meticulous in her work. In those days, there were not many well-educated women. So the supervisor promoted her to the office to work as a clerk overseeing the warehouse and the accounts. Through wisdom given by God, she performed very well in her work and was highly regarded by her superiors and fellow workers.

Nevertheless, this rosy scene did not last very long. When

the Cultural Revolution broke out, as the family of a counter-revolutionary, HuiZhen and her children suffered.

One day, when HuiZhen stepped into the office, it was plastered with posters that read, 'The family member of a counter-revolutionary is not allowed to hold a high position in a company!' 'Send the family member of the counter-revolutionary to the front line to a corrective work order!' Though her name was not mentioned, it was obvious whom the posters were referring to.

The next day, her superior said to her, 'From today onwards, you are transferred back to the construction site.' HuiZhen did not say anything but just nodded. From then on her work kept changing and the workload kept increasing. In the beginning, she was assigned to transporting bricks on a small trolley, and was required to complete a trip every fifteen minutes, carrying 150 bricks each trip (altogether 375kg in weight). Later, she had to sift sand, and then to mix cement with stones for concrete. These were the toughest jobs on the construction site. Her whole body would become soaked with sweat. During winter, she had to endure the icy-cold wind. But regardless of the conditions, her superior demanded that she complete her allotted work on time. When she got home from work she had to take care of the family and she often worked till late at night. In order to save money, she altered Yuan's clothes for the older children and the older children's clothes for the younger ones. She often stayed up late to complete these tailoring jobs. Once, while she was out visiting a friend, her mother-in-law fell and broke her leg and was bedridden, so HuiZhen stayed at home to take care of her.

She could endure the heavy workload and the financial pressures through tight management and longsuffering, but the political pressures she found extremely difficult to bear.

Because of her links with a counter-revolutionary, nothing she did was appreciated and she was forced to endure the contempt of everyone. When her group received an award for excellent performance at work, she was the only one deprived of the award. The head of the group purposely passed over her, even though she had done most of the work in the group. Her children also had to suffer. FuSheng, the third child, was due to have been assigned work in a bicycle factory but the school retained the letter of notification issued by the factory for him. They said, 'Those who have prisoners as family members cannot stay in Beijing.' So FuSheng was sent to work at the arsenal in Ningxia, only returning to Beijing after nine years. PingHu, the fifth child, was a young woman with great integrity who performed well in her work. But she was discriminated against because of her counter-revolutionary father. She was not allowed to participate in the national-day parade and was treated as if she was a criminal. She was spoken of highly by her colleagues for her hard work and excellent performance but her name never appeared on the list of good workers compiled by her superior. Her superior asked her, 'Do you know why your name does not appear on the list of good workers?' She said, 'It's because of my father, isn't it?' Some of the workers felt that she was unjustly treated and fought for her rights. They talked to the superior, 'Yuan HuPing should not be blamed for her family background. She did not choose to be born into that family. She's performing very well in her work. Why don't you include her on the list of good workers?' The superior said, 'As a member of a counter-revolutionary family, she's already being treated very well. At least she still has a job and is still paid. What more can she ask for?' This was the policy towards the families of counter-revolutionaries in those days.

As the persecutions of the Cultural Revolution stepped up, HuiZhen's difficulties intensified. For about six months, she was criticised every day. Nineteen members of her unit were assigned to repudiate her on a daily basis. They took turns interrogating HuiZhen and heaped immense mental pressure on her. They started by trying to force her to turn against her faith. They said, 'If you believe in Jesus, you're opposing the proletariat, and you'll suffer serious consequences. If you renounce your faith in Jesus, we'll take you into the Communist Party. If only you would publicly renounce your faith, all your sufferings would end immediately.' Besides this, they tried to force her to divorce her husband so that she could draw a line between herself and this counter-revolutionary. When they discovered that she was still in touch with her husband in the prison, they warned her sternly, 'If you still keep in touch with that counter-revolutionary, we'll deal with you severely.' HuiZhen stopped visiting Yuan during this period but she never gave up her faith or her husband. Those who criticised her wracked their brains for all kinds of ways to coerce her. One day, they accused her of misappropriating funds. HuiZhen was puzzled – she had never imagined that they would stoop to such a dirty trick. She said, 'I have not misappropriated even one cent.' They argued, 'We've collected ample evidence to charge you. We'll give you a chance. If you own up, we won't deal with you as severely as if you resist. You'd better think very carefully.' HuiZhen insisted, 'I've never even taken one cent.' She began to fear that by being so insistent she might add fuel to their fire, but she suddenly remembered the words of Scripture, *'If you falter in times of trouble, how small is your strength!'* (Proverbs 24:10). So she continued to defend herself courageously. They did not give up. They tried to blackmail her by saying, 'If you won't own up, we'll take this matter further.' HuiZhen repeatedly denied any wrongdoing.

HuiZhen did not give into their coercion, however hard they tried. In the daytime, she had to work and endure criticism; at night, she prayed to the Lord in tears. In these agonising days, she drew near to the Lord, and the Lord granted her the peace that surpasses all understanding. After six months of futile efforts to slander her, they finally gave up because of lack of evidence. Another member of her group who had undergone similar treatment had lost his sanity. HuiZhen knew that if it were not for God's protection, she would have committed suicide or gone mad. Throughout those six months, she never saw a smiling face or met with a pair of helping hands.

One day, her group leader who had been slandering her told her, 'Now that you have been found innocent, you still have to carry on the revolution by accusing others.' HuiZhen realised that in those days, accusing others was a way of gaining political benefits. If she would accuse others, she would be included in the 'slandering task force' and could avenge her accusers. But her Christian conscience forbade her to take any part in it and reminded her always to walk according to the ways of the Lord. She answered the group leader, 'All I know is that I'm not involved in corruption. I don't know about anyone else. I won't slander others.'

At the end of six months, having failed to make any of their accusations against her stick, they ended their criticism of her completely. Her group leader summoned her to the office and said, 'After looking into the matter in detail, we find that you don't have any problem. Let's forget what happened in the past and turn over a new leaf. The company has decided to restore you to your previous position.' Thus, her two years of unjust treatment had ended officially.

When Yuan was arrested, HuiZhen was not yet forty; she looked younger than her age and she was still quite pretty. When Yuan was sentenced to life imprisonment some of her friends who were sympathetic towards her advised her to divorce and remarry. They said to her, 'Now that your husband has been sentenced to life imprisonment, why should you put up with all this baggage of being a counter-revolutionary family?', and some of them tried to act as matchmakers for her. Many men also tried their best to woo her, using all kinds of excuses to approach her. Some of them tried to attract her through their wealth, and one or two even wrote a divorce certificate for her. She was, however, very firm. 'Stop all these silly efforts,' she would say. 'When my unit tried to coerce me to divorce, I didn't give in. I won't consider divorce and remarriage.'

However, this was all a great trial for HuiZhen whose priority was taking care of her six children. When Yuan was in prison, she was virtually a widow and the children were virtually orphans. But however difficult it was, God strengthened her and helped her to resist all temptations so that she continued to be faithful to her marriage covenant.

Throughout this difficult period, HuiZhen's firm faith saw her through as she passed from middle age into old age. The prayers of her fellow brothers and sisters in Christ had sustained her.

After Yuan's arrest, the wife of his old teacher, Mrs Wang, visited HuiZhen frequently. Mr Wang KeChen had helped Yuan to rent the Gospel Hall in Fuchengmen, Beijing. Mrs Wang was a housewife and loved the Lord. Their son, who was originally an Orthopaedic doctor at the Jishuitan Hospital, had been transferred to Huairou because of his faith, but he continued to hold fast to Jesus. HuiZhen also visited their house to pray with Mrs Wang. Apart from them, Liu ShuJie was HuiZhen's other close friend during this period. Liu ShuJie was the wife of Yang JinGuang, who had been sent for a corrective work order in Chadian because of his association with the Wang MingDao counter-revolutionary syndicate. Yuan met JinGuang in Chadian in 1962. When she visited HuiZhen and asked what she could do for her, HuiZhen replied, 'I'm glad that you've come to see me. I'm OK. I've got a job and enough money. Income is not a problem.' After Yuan was transferred to the North-east in 1966, Liu ShuJie said to HuiZhen in tears, 'I'll cancel my day off on Sundays from now onwards. Tell me when you're going to the North-east to visit your husband and I'll go with you.' HuiZhen was very touched. She was the only one who was not afraid to visit Yuan in prison.

In those days, two blind Christians, Chen BangHeng and Zhang YongHe, also visited HuiZhen frequently. One Saturday afternoon, Chen BangHeng called in. He told HuiZhen, 'Last night, I dreamed about Rev. Yuan. He came back and preached from the pulpit. Has he come back?' HuiZhen replied, 'No, he hasn't.' But she was very grateful to God for caring for her and her family through these believers. Chen BangHeng was very talented in singing and often led her whole family in singing hymns, such as 'Wait, wait. Don't worry', to comfort them.

On one occasion, HuiZhen gave 100 dollars that she had saved to a brother in Christ in difficult circumstances. The next day, she herself was in need of money. Meanwhile, a man sent 600 dollars to her which had been given to him by a Christian woman who knew her situation. At that time, her monthly salary was about thirty dollars. She donated one tenth of it to help a couple, Mr and Mrs Zhang FuYuan, who had no children. Even in her darkest hour, she never stopped giving one tenth of her income to the Lord.

HuiZhen insisted on visiting Mrs Wang and praying with her once a month. Mrs Wang was a woman of great faith. She said, 'O Lord, I believe that before I pass away, I'll be able to see Yuan return. I'm confident that he will continue to serve the Lord.' HuiZhen prayed, 'I pray that in whatever circumstances he is in, You will strengthen Yuan, so that he will persevere to the end and will not stumble and compromise when he thinks of us. Help him to honour Your name and persevere to the end.'

In her darkest moments, HuiZhen experienced the love and faithfulness of God. She always said, 'Our brothers and sisters really love us very much. I feel unworthy of their love.' God demonstrated His faithfulness in the life of a frail woman:

> *'A father to the fatherless, a defender of widows,*
> *is God in his holy dwelling.*
> *God sets the lonely in families,*
> *he leads forth the prisoners with singing . . . '*

(Psalm 68:5–6)

PART VII

*'They who hope in the Lord
will renew their strength'*

Chapter 19

On Parole

In 1979, China entered a new era of reformation and openness which focused on economic development. Deng XiaoPing was by this time officially in power, and he began to introduce a series of ideological, political and economic reforms and to review the extreme left-wing policies of the past. His reformation was known as the 'Restoration of Order and Return to the Right Path'. As part of this process he also began to redress unjust court cases, and many who had been categorised as right-wingers, including religious leaders, were released. At that time, Yuan was still in prison in the North-east. He did not realise that God's new plan for him had already begun to unfold.

In the latter half of 1979, China began to loosen up its policies, and the situation was much less tense than it had been in the 1950s and 1960s. The prison in the North-east was suffering from overcrowding and the old prisoners who could no longer work were becoming a burden for the government. In order to cut down on expenses, the government decided to release men who were sixty years and over as well as those who had been imprisoned for more than twenty years. These prisoners were being released in batches. Those who did not have a home were assigned work. The government made this decision to release the counter-revolutionaries for two reasons. Firstly, most of them had been unjustly charged or punished and were not nearly as dangerous as had been propagated for political advantage: they were political scapegoats. Some had even been sentenced for just a few remarks they had made. Secondly, over the past twenty years, society had changed beyond recognition. There was no longer room for counter-revolution and counter-revolutionaries no longer posed any danger to society. In the latter half of 1979, the First Prison in Heilongjiang began to release older prisoners. When Yuan heard this news, he said to himself, 'I meet the conditions for release. Could it be that God wants me to serve Him again?' But he doubted that it could possibly be true. When it was finally confirmed that the government did indeed have such a policy, he wrote a letter to his family in order to give them a chance to prepare themselves mentally. The letter read, 'Lord willing, perhaps I'll be released shortly.' When HuiZhen received the letter, she was overjoyed, but she could not believe it could possibly be true. It was not surprising that they should be so sceptical, as it really was a huge change-round in government policy. God worked on their behalf when they were least expecting it.

HuiZhen was afraid that it might just be a rumour circulating in the prison. In order to make sure, she asked FuYin to write a letter to the Intermediate People's Court in Beijing for official confirmation. She did not know that these reforms were still at an early stage, and communication and links between the various bureaux had not yet been properly established. She thought the best line of approach would be to consult the court, but in actual fact the Penitentiary Department notified the various prisons about the release of prisoners before it informed the courts. FuYin's letter to the Intermediate People's Court read, 'I'm the son of Yuan, who was arrested in April 1958. I'm not sure what offence he committed to deserve such a severe punishment, but I know that many similar cases have been redressed. I feel that my father was punished unfairly. Is it possible for my father's case to be redressed?' Two weeks later, the court summoned FuYin to an interview. He was interviewed by a woman who, after asking his name and occupation, said, 'Your father's case is quite complicated. I cannot give any guarantees. His situation is similar to Wang MingDao's. Both are leaders of a counter-revolutionary syndicate. His sentence was appropriate. It will not be redressed.' FuYin said, 'However complicated his case, you must spell out the rationale behind it clearly. Without doing so, how can you justify the sentence given in 1958?' The woman saw that he was emotionally very fraught and said to him, 'You had no say about the family into which you were born, but you can choose your own pathway in life. Don't get yourself associated with counter-revolution; just focus on your work.' FuYin said, 'I do understand my father's situation. I'm his eldest son. I was seventeen years old when he was arrested. I knew that he had not committed any crime. I want to know why he was accused of counter-revolution. Wasn't Liu ShaoQi accused of counter-revolution, too? But now his case has been redressed. If you could make a mistake in sentencing the president, you could also make a mistake in the case of other people.' The interviewer became incensed and said, 'Don't link your father to Liu ShaoQi. Liu ShaoQi is Liu ShaoQi; your father is your father. Their two cases are very different. Your father's sentence is appropriate. There is no mistake. This discussion is fruitless; we should end it here.' She handed FuYin a copy of the court's formal reply. The letter, which was dated 16 November 1979, read, 'Yuan Fu Yin, we have received your letter. After looking into the matter, we conclude that our sentence on Yuan in case no. 1013 in 1958 was appropriate.'

After reading the letter, FuYin returned home with a heavy heart. When he arrived home, HuiZhen asked impatiently, 'What did they say?' FuYin handed her the letter. After reading it, she sighed, 'Trust the Lord. All we can do is wait.' After this incident, none of them in the family believed that Yuan would ever be released, and so they did not prepare themselves mentally for that possibility.

After a few days, FuSheng's wife told him, 'I saw your father in my dream. He had returned.' On hearing this, FuSheng smiled, but made no comment and did not think any more about it. At that time, they lived in a small house they had built near his mother's house. It was six metres square.

FuSheng's wife had never met her father-in-law, and FuSheng thought that she had had the dream because she had heard recently that his father might be released. But now the family had all resigned themselves to the fact that it was not going to happen.

On 20 December 1979, when Yuan was eating lunch after work, the chief warder came to make an announcement. All of the prisoners stood up. At that time, announcements about the release of prisoners were being made every day. More than thirty prisoners from their farm had already been released. On that day, Yuan's name was included in the list. Yuan was very surprised. However, he had not completely ruled out the possibility, and had begun to prepare himself mentally for it. He was excited but not exuberant – perhaps decades of imprisonment had made him numb. His excitement began to grow gradually. The chief warder told them to finish their meal quickly. After lunch, Yuan packed his belongings. Some of them he threw away, the rest he gave away. Before their release, each of the prisoners was given a set of black clothes for the journey home, as well as sixty dollars for their fare. The chief warder asked Yuan where he lived. Yuan replied, 'White Pagoda Street in Beijing.' On hearing this, he said, 'It is not permitted for you to establish residency in the five cities of China (Beijing, Shanghai, Nanjing, Guangzhou and Tianjin). Do you have any children living in smaller cities? You can establish residency there.' Yuan wrote down the address of his eldest son, who lived in Shijingshan, Beijing, which he recalled was farming land. When he was writing the address, he suddenly remembered that he had not met FuYin's wife. How could he live with them? But he had no choice. Afterwards, he wrote a letter to his family telling them he was being released, and sent it by registered mail. He was so happy that he could not sleep.

That afternoon, he was no longer required to work. He could not wait to go home. Early the next day, each of them was given a certificate of release from the prison. When he looked at the address on the certificate, he was very glad that it was White Pagoda Street, not Shijingshan.

The certificate of release that Yuan received was actually a certificate of parole, number 665/1979, issued by the Superior People's Court of Heilongjiang. The certificate read, 'Yuan's release on parole is effective from the date stated above until 3 October 1989. While on parole, he is deprived of all political privileges.' Only after completion of his ten-year parole could Yuan apply for citizenship. During that time, he had to apply for a permit from the police station if he wanted to leave Beijing and, in addition, his thought would be subject to regular scrutiny.

When Yuan received his certificate of parole on 21 December 1979, he immediately set off for home. He walked the three kilometres from the prison to the taxi stand and took a taxi to Gezhi City, where he caught a train. Because Gezhi was a small town, there was no express train. The train stopped at Heilongjiang, Jilin and Liaoning before arriving in Beijing. Because of the cold weather, the steam engine could not function properly and so it was a very slow journey. The slow-moving train made him even more impatient to get home. When the train stopped at Taipingchuan Station in Jilin, he got off and changed to an express train to Beijing. He could not wait to see his family, so he did not mind spending the extra money. Having bought a ticket he sent a telegram home telling his family to meet him at the railway station at 10.30 p.m. on 23 December. Having arrived at the post office after 5.00 p.m., when it was just about to close, he could only send a few words. The telegram read, 'I'm taking a train on 22 December. I'll arrive at 10.30 p.m. on 23 Dec.' The officer did not remind him that he had forgotten to write his name. When HuiZhen received the telegram that afternoon, she could not think who had sent it. The address indicated that it had been sent from Taipingchuan, Jilin, a place unknown to her. She could not figure out who in the world would send a telegram from there. That evening, one of FuSheng's friends came to visit him. His wife was from the North-east and had stayed with HuiZhen for a month when she had been in Beijing for medical treatment. So HuiZhen asked him, 'Is this telegram from your wife? There was no name on it.' He said, 'No, it's

not from my wife; she's here.' FuSheng suddenly had an idea
... He said, 'Mum, perhaps it's from Dad.' HuiZhen thought,
'Yuan is very forgetful. It is not uncommon for him to forget
to put his name. But the address is incorrect. He's in
Heilongjiang, not Jilin.' FuSheng found a train schedule.
He said excitedly, 'Yes! It must be from Dad. You see, look
at the train route ... from Gezhi to Taipingchuan, and
from Taipingchuan to Beijing. Dad must have taken a train
at Taipingchuan. He'll be here tomorrow.' On hearing this,
HuiZhen's face beamed with joy. But then doubt began to set
in again. 'It's very unlikely. We just received notice from the
court on 16 November that his case would not be redressed.'
Their joy soon evaporated again, for they believed the letter
issued by the court was much more likely to be reliable than
any other possibility. But any way they would still go to the
train station.

On the afternoon of 23 December, when FuSheng came
home from work, he saw a letter addressed to his mother and
he recognised his father's handwriting. He opened the envelope immediately. The letter sent from the prison read, 'I'm
coming back. Get ready for my return. I'll send a telegram to
let you know the date.' On reading this, tears of excitement
streamed down his cheeks. When HuiZhen returned from her
office at 5.30 p.m., FuSheng rushed out of the house exclaim-
ing, 'Mum, this is Dad's letter. Didn't I tell you that Dad was
coming back? But you wouldn't believe it. Look, this is his
letter.' They read the letter together a few more times, with
tears streaming down their cheeks. FuSheng's wife urged
them to eat their dinner quickly so that they could get to
the station early. That evening, none of them had any
appetite. They only ate some porridge before they went
o the railway station. FuSheng went to tell AnHu and PingHu
the good news. That night, HuiZhen, FuSheng and AnHu and
her husband, Zhang ZhongXian, went to the railway station
to meet Yuan. They stood at the only four exits of the railway
station and waited from 8.30 p.m. till midnight. They saw
streams of people, but they did not see Yuan.

They waited for four hours until the railway station was
almost empty and was about to close. But they refused to

leave. They asked the officer, 'Has any train been delayed?'
He replied, 'No. All the trains have arrived and all the
passengers have left. There's no point waiting here. Go
home.'

Tired, disappointed and helpless, they stood in the cold
north wind. Nobody uttered a word. HuiZhen could not hold
back her tears. She kept praying, 'O God, what's happened?'
AnHu sighed, 'I'm afraid something might have happened to
Dad to stop him returning...' They were overcome with
grief. A short time ago, they had been so excited; now they
were plunged into despair. This emotional rollercoaster
exhausted them.

AnHu was worried about her mother, so she said, 'Mum,
why don't you come and stay with me tonight? We'll come
again tomorrow.' HuiZhen said, 'No. I've got to go to work
tomorrow.' AnHu said, 'Why don't you take a taxi home? It's
more convenient.' HuiZhen, 'No, it's too expensive. I'll take a
bus home with FuSheng.' So they took a bus home. Nobody
said anything. The bus stopped at Xisi, where AnHu and her
husband lived. Then HuiZhen and FuSheng walked home
from Xisi.

All the way home HuiZhen kept looking around, hoping to
see Yuan. Perhaps he had made his own way home and got
lost. The nearer home she got, the more depressed she felt.
When she arrived home, she broke down in tears and asked
God once again, 'O God, what's happened? The joy was so
short-lived.'

FuSheng was at a loss for words to comfort his mother.
When he looked up, he saw that the light in his mother's
room was on. As an economical person, HuiZhen would not
have left it on. In any case, he had seen his mother switch the
light off before they left the house. And it was unlikely that
his wife would be in his mother's room so late at night.
Could it be that his father had returned? HuiZhen also saw
the light. They looked at each other, but did not say
anything. When they opened the door, they saw a bald
man washing his feet. It was Yuan!

When Yuan recognised his wife and son, he immediately
got up with his feet still in the basin of water, and reached

out his hands to them. They hugged each other and wept. Yuan said, 'You've suffered throughout these years.'

When FuSheng's wife heard the noise, she came out from her room and saw them crying. She, too, could not hold back her tears. She thought that they should be happy, not sad, about Yuan's return, so she tried to cheer them up. She said, 'Look at yourself, FuSheng. How silly you are. Your father has come home.' On hearing this, they all burst out laughing.

But how did they manage to miss Yuan?

Yuan's train was delayed. It was supposed to have arrived at 10.30 p.m., but it had not arrived until after 11.00 p.m. The lamps at the exits were dim, so they could not see clearly, and Yuan was wearing black clothes and a hat, so they had not recognised him. He should have recognised them, but, because of his impatience, when he had not seen them at the exit, he had thought that either they had not received his telegram or they had already gone home. Actually, had he looked closer or turned back, he would have seen them. After he had left the railway station, he had wanted to take a 103 bus, but when he had found they were no longer running he had decided to take a taxi home even though it would cost a bit more. But just as he was about to take a taxi, two men had come to the bus stop and he had heard one of them say, 'I'm going to White Pagoda Temple. As there are no more 103 buses, I'll take a late night bus.' So Yuan had changed his mind and followed the man to another bus stop to wait for the late night bus. Yuan had also got off at the Xisi bus stop. Because he had had no coins, he had given the bus conductor ten dollars, but as he had had no change either, he had returned the money to Yuan. After he had got off the bus, he had headed west towards the White Pagoda Temple, thinking he would find the house when he saw the temple, but the temple had been demolished and he had gone too far. He had kept walking north, shouting HuiZhen's name as he walked, but no one had responded. He had seen a house with a light still on, so he had gone up to the house and shouted HuiZhen's name. FuSheng's wife, who had fallen asleep while waiting for their return, had been awakened by Yuan's shout. When she had heard somebody calling her mother-in-law's name, she had responded from the house, 'My mother has gone to the railway station. What's the matter?' Yuan had said, 'She has gone to the railway station to meet me.' On hearing this, she had rushed out but when she had seen her father-in-law for the first time, she had been at a loss for words. She had introduced herself as his daughter-in-law, brought him into the house and fetched basins for him to wash his face and feet. That was when HuiZhen and FuSheng had arrived.

At long last, Yuan had returned safely. He had been absent for twenty-one years and eight months. When he was arrested, the children were still very young. Now they had grown up. When he was arrested, his mother had still been alive, now he could only look at her photograph. During these twenty-one years, the responsibility for the whole family had rested on the frail shoulders of HuiZhen.

> *'Blessed is the man who perseveres under trial ... he will receive the crown of life.'*   (James 1:12)

God had accomplished an unimaginable feat through Yuan's family.

In the early part of his ministry, Yuan had thought that having a family would be a help to his ministry and so he had not considered staying single. He had believed that as a servant of the Lord caring for the ministry of the Lord, the Lord would take care of his family. This had been the grace of God. His twenty-one years in prison had deprived his family of his care. He wasn't there to nurture his children when they were in need or serve his mother during her last days. But HuiZhen had accomplished what he had not been able to do. When he was in prison, he had received a monthly allowance of 2.50 dollars, which he had sent home. There had been tension in Yuan's relationship with his parents after his conversion, but he had always tried to honour them, and their relationship had improved after his mother's conversion. After Yuan's arrest, his mother had said to HuiZhen, 'When my son was here, I didn't have very good food. Now that he has been imprisoned and I've got to live on you, I don't expect good food either. I'm content with whatever I have and I look to the Lord. I don't mind enduring a difficult life with you; whatever you eat I'll eat. But I feel sorry that you've got to take care of so many children.' HuiZhen said, 'You're not living on me because we're all living on God.' Her mother-in-law had been given the gift of healing after her conversion. She had laid hands on Mrs Li and had prayed for her healing and her diarrhoea had been cured. She had often visited others until she had become senile when she was eighty years old. She lived with her daughter-in-law until she passed away at age eighty-two. Throughout these twenty-one years, HuiZhen had built a warm family with the wisdom given by God.

Yuan asked HuiZhen, 'How did you endure these twenty-one years?' She answered, 'The greater the problem, the greater God's grace.'

After his release, Yuan told his children, 'You were still young when I was arrested. Now that you have grown up, I want you to understand that there are two ways you can choose. You've got to choose one of them.' FuYin and FuLe were the first to be born again. AnHu and PingHu were baptised later. This was a great comfort to Yuan. These six children were all very respectful and none of them had gone off the rails. Yuan was very grateful to the Lord for this. He said, 'I sing hallelujah every day.'

Yuan led a very disciplined life. He was very wise in his preaching of the Word. He relied on the Lord and not man. Concerning future church leadership, he always believed that the Lord chose His own servants. He did his best to train young leaders and, as long as a young man was eager, he would train him.

FuYin was baptised in the Three-Self Church in Gangwa City in 1980, having discussed his decision with his father beforehand. His father had said, 'You must decide for yourself. I'm glad that you want to be baptised. But this is between you and God. You must first of all understand the will of God.' The church wanted him to join the Three-Self Movement after his baptism, but he refused. He told them that he could not agree with them. They approached him again, but he insisted that he would not change his mind. He said, 'I've been considered a counter-revolutionary since I was young. I'm not afraid. I have different views to the Three-Self Movement.' Eventually, they gave up. Yuan had never demanded that his children be baptised. He wanted them to be sure of their salvation and let them choose baptism of their own free will. But he cared about their spirituality and their philosophy of life.

The government had released counter-revolutionaries like him because it believed that through the changes of the last twenty years counter-revolutionary thoughts had become outdated. The government was partially right. In terms of daily living, Yuan was indeed out of date. On his release from prison he had been given sixty dollars and he had said happily to HuiZhen, 'I've brought sixty dollars for you', not realising it was no longer a large amount of money. HuiZhen said, 'I don't want your money. I want you.' He had also brought a blanket home but it was so worn out that she threw it away. Yuan smiled and said, 'If I had known that my house was so big, I wouldn't have brought this rubbish home.' When he had been arrested, Shijingshan was still a farming village. It had now become a city and there was a steel factory on what was once farm land. HuiZhen cooked all kinds of good food for him after his release, but he still felt that the chicken raised on a traditional farm was better than that from a modern farm. So he asked FuYin to buy some chicken from a traditional farm in Shijingshan. FuYin said, 'Dad, there is no longer a traditional farm in Shijingshan. Even people in Shijingshan are eating chickens raised on a modern farm.'

In the matter of religion, the government was wrong. For God is the same yesterday, today and forever. Religious truth would never become outdated.

When he was released, Yuan was approaching sixty-six. One of his neighbours was very concerned about how he would earn a living. He asked him, 'Now that you're old, you may find it very difficult to get a job. Why don't you work as a newspaper vendor or security guard? I can help you.' Yuan was very grateful for his kindness, but he declined his offer. He was afraid that his children might not be happy about it either. After Yang JinGuang had been released, he continued to work in the hospital. He was also concerned about Yuan's future. He said to Yuan, 'They need translators for the religious sections of the encyclopaedia. Since your English is so good, you can work as a translator to earn a living. You don't need to go to an office. You can work at home.' Yuan said, 'No. I'm not prepared to work any more. Now that my wife and children are working, our livelihood is not a problem. I want to grasp the opportunity to serve God, to make up for what I've missed in the past.'

A few days after his return, HuiZhen took him to see his old teacher, Wang KeChen, and his wife. They were the first Christians he visited after his release. Mrs Wang had prayed earnestly for Yuan when he had been in prison and had believed that he would be released before her death. Now she was blind. HuiZhen asked her, 'Mrs Wang, guess whom I have brought to see you?' Mrs Wang reached out her hand and held Yuan's hand. Yuan said, 'Mrs Wang, I'm Yuan. I've come to see you.' Mrs Wang could not believe her ears. She asked, 'Are you really Yuan?' Yuan said, 'It's really me. I'm back.' This time Mrs Wang recognised his voice. She was so excited that tears ran down her cheeks. She grasped Yuan's hand and said, 'The Lord has truly answered my prayer. He is a faithful God. He let me live till ninety years old to witness how He has answered my prayer.' Mrs Wang passed away at age ninety-six.

The second Christian that Yuan visited was HuiZhen's younger sister who had been a backslidden Christian for more than two decades. She was very touched by Yuan's faithfulness to the Lord throughout his two decades in prison. She said, 'Actually, I was a believer, but I did not dare to admit it during the Cultural Revolution. Now I want to trust the Lord again.'

Four of Yuan's six children were in Beijing but FuLe, who had visited Yuan in Gezhi in 1977, worked in Guizhou and XiaoLiu worked in Datong, Shanxi. She was the only child that Yuan had not seen for fourteen years. Yuan decided to

visit XiaoLiu and her family in Datong. He went before the
Chinese New Year of 1980 and stayed there until the end
of Chinese New Year. When he arrived at Datong railway
station, XiaoLiu and her husband were there to meet him.
They stood at the two exits of the station. XiaoLiu's husband
saw someone looking for somebody, and guessed that that
person might be his father-in-law. He approached the person
and discovered that it was really the person that they had
been waiting for. So he took Yuan to find XiaoLiu. XiaoLiu
felt that her father had turned very dark and skinny now. She
took leave from work in order to be with him. He shared
the gospel with her friends and two of them accepted the
Lord.

After Yuan's release, he was faced with two choices. One
was to join the Three-Self Movement. By so doing, he would
receive a lot of benefits, including a pension. Leaders of
the Three-Self Movement approached him and said that the
Movement was open to him. The other choice was to stay in
the House Church Movement. He chose the latter. A number
of Christians advised him, 'Many cases have been redressed
now. You should also seek for redress.' Yuan knew that he
had been falsely accused, but he refused to seek redress. He
said, 'The Bible says that we should back down for the Lord
Himself is the avenger. The Lord Jesus did not answer back
when He was mocked. He trusted God, the righteous Judge.
What I've suffered is insignificant in comparison with the
Lord's suffering.' One pastor told him, 'You should put your
defence in writing. You may be able to rid your family of
the label of counter-revolutionary, and your children will
benefit.' He replied, 'I should have died, but the Lord has
redeemed me. I should spend the rest of my life serving
Him. I haven't got time to write letters defending myself.
The authority of God is greater than any label of counter-
revolutionary. I don't care what label they put on me.'

Chapter 20

Establishing Residency

One of Yuan's first tasks after his release was to establish residency in Beijing. China was very strict on population control, particularly in order to keep people from flocking to the big cities. If he did not manage to establish residency, life would be very inconvenient for him. Establishing residency turned out to be a wonderful experience for Yuan.

In those days, establishing residency was a very complicated procedure in Beijing. One needed a letter of recommendation and certification from a committee member of the Communist Party. HuiZhen had retired in 1979 but was later hired as an assessor in an engineering firm, where she was highly regarded for her work. She said to her superior, 'My husband wants to establish residency.' Her superior said, 'OK, you've contributed a lot to our firm. I'll see to it.' HuiZhen wrote down the date of Yuan's release, the name of his prison, and the place where he wanted to establish residency. Her superior then submitted his application to the police station. One month after Yuan's return, on 23 January 1980, it was approved. On that day, when HuiZhen returned home from work, a policeman came to the house and told her, 'The application for Beijing residency by Mr Yuan has been approved.' Yuan went to the police station to get the certificate of residency. He showed the officer his certificate of parole and, after they had looked into his situation for a moment, they handed him the certificate of residency along with coupons for cloth, food and oil. It went very smoothly. This was indeed the grace of God. About twenty of the people with him at the police station did not get their application approved, even though some of them had been applying for years. Many people wanted residency in Beijing because they wanted a better job in the city. Yuan did not need this for his children were supporting him, but God granted what he did not request.

Many of his friends called HuiZhen at her office after they found out that he had successfully received official residency, asking her how they had managed to achieve it so easily. She answered, 'It's very easy. You get a letter of recommendation from your unit and tell the policeman where the applicant served his prison term.' People would say, 'But it didn't work for me.' In those days, it was indeed a miracle to be able to establish residency in Beijing successfully. The son of Wu MuJia also came to see HuiZhen and said, 'My Dad's application for residency in Beijing was turned down, so he had to establish residency at my sister's place in Inner Mongolia. But how did Yuan get his so easily?' HuiZhen answered, 'This is the grace of God. He moved my superior to give me a letter of recommendation. There was no bribery and no strings attached at all.'

Now Yuan had established residency, but was not yet a citizen. He was not allowed to apply for citizenship for ten years because the police did not trust him. Without citizenship, he was not allowed to leave Beijing and had to report to the police station twice a month. The police rejected his appeal to report only once a month because of his 'criminal' record. When he reported to the police station he was required to hand in an essay. Having written such reports for years, he was very experienced. There were three main points to his essays:

1. transformation of the mind through reading the newspaper and listening to broadcasts;
2. cooking at home;
3. looking forward to being granted citizenship.

He repeated these three points in all his essays until the policeman was so tired of it he asked him not to hand in any more. The police had the neighbours observe Yuan, but he was on good terms with them. Later, they only required him to write a summary annually and then he copied a few paragraphs from the newspaper for his summary. Finally, he did not even need to write a summary. At the end of 1989, a policeman came and said, 'The end of your parole is near. Write a summary.' After the police had approved his summary and stamped it, they sent it to the First Prison of Heilongjiang for approval. Thus, Yuan was completely released and he received his identity card in October 1989.

Chapter 21

Back to the Ministry

While Yuan was away in Datong in 1980 visiting XiaoLiu, a Mr Zhao from Hong Kong came to visit him in Beijing. He introduced himself as a kindergarten teacher, and said that he had heard the news of Yuan's release from a radio broadcast. In the broadcast Yuan had been reported as still having black hair and being as strong and energetic as when he was young. He had come to check this out. He unfortunately missed Yuan, but HuiZhen was able to confirm the news. He was the first foreigner to visit Yuan after his release.[1] As the news of his release spread, he began to receive many more visits from foreign Christians and this took up quite a lot of his time.

After his release, Yuan had a strong desire to continue his ministry, and this was why he declined offers for other jobs. Many believers visited him and asked him questions about the Bible and prayed with him. Yuan wanted to make the most of the time he had left, so he said to them, 'Why don't we start a Bible study on Wednesdays?' Later, he even began a Sunday worship service. In the spring of 1980, there were about ten people attending his house meetings.

An important part of his ministry included distributing the Bible. In 1981 the Three-Self Movement had not yet begun to print the Bible, but that year Yuan sent out more than two thousand copies. The copies were provided by a pastor from Hong Kong and the Open Doors Ministry – a parachurch organisation involved in sending Bibles into restricted access countries. Later, a group of visitors from the US who attended Yuan's meeting and heard his testimony also sent copies of the Bible to Chinese Christians through him. Giving out the Bible was illegal in those days, but Yuan was not afraid. He said, 'How shall they worship the Lord without the Bible?' Yuan also had XiaoLiu take some Bibles to Datong and distribute them to the believers there. She was interrogated by the leaders of the Three-Self Movement but, thank God, they did not give her any trouble.

Yuan's children contributed a lot to the work of distributing Christian literature. PingHu received the literature on Yuan's behalf three times. Because Yuan was always out and the books were very heavy, they were sent to PingHu. One afternoon, two policemen and a policewoman came to PingHu's home looking for Yuan but he wasn't there. They asked her how many books there were in the box. She answered, 'I've got no idea. I haven't opened the box.' One of them said, 'All this is subversive literature sent from foreign countries. We can actually arrest you and bring you to the station for interrogation. But we'll give you a chance. We'll go to your office and talk to them about this.' To safeguard your future, you'd better co-operate with us.' One of them by the name of Mr Yang said, 'I've known your father for more than ten years.' He had been the policeman in charge of Yuan's case all that time. He said, 'If he wants to have house meetings, we won't stop him. But we won't allow this literature. It's a serious matter that we need to deal with.' After that, they asked her some questions and made a note of her answers. Finally, they said, 'There are many religious fanatics carrying out their anti-Communist activities in your father's name. Your father is a good man with a sincere religious faith. He's just like Mao Zedong, who in his old age was being made use of by people like JiangQing. People are trying to make use of your father in the same way now. You're still young; you'd better look out for your father's interests. Next time, if someone sends any books to you, remember to inform us immediately. We'll deal with it. If you receive books, you can open up the parcel and have a look. If they are appropriate for distribution, distribute them.

If not, we'll deal with them.' PingHu did not reply. They asked again, 'To whom have you distributed these books?' She answered, 'I gave them to my father; I haven't looked at them. I've got no idea what's inside the box.' They asked her to sign her name on an acknowledgement book and left. Afterwards, they interrogated her superior at her place of work. Her superior said, 'Yuan HuPing has been with us for a long time and is now the chairman of our labour union. She is an honest woman. I don't think she's involved in any offence.' They said, 'We're not getting at her, but her father. The Communist Party imprisoned him for more than twenty years. Do you think he won't have any grudges against the Party?' Her superior said, 'I've heard that her father is more than eighty now and his eyesight is diminishing. Come on, what can he do now?' Having achieved nothing, they left.

Yuan tried various methods of evangelism. He bought a video recorder to make videos for the believers. His main target was the older women who were illiterate. In order to improve his rural evangelism, he made use of a slide projector. The slide projectors made in China were very cheap and easy to use. However, the process of making the slides was tedious and time consuming. In the beginning, Yuan and some co-workers drew some pictures depicting Bible stories such as the prodigal son and also the Gospel Bridge, illustrating how to become a Christian. But when someone gave them a few sets of ready-made slides, they stopped producing their own. There were not many pastors in the House Church Movement, so Yuan recorded his own preaching and distributed it to other house churches. He also distributed sermon tapes received from overseas.

In the beginning of his house church ministry, the government did not interfere, because the number of participants was very limited. During his parole, they met in the houses of other believers and that was why his ministry escaped the notice of the police and his neighbours.

In 1986, there were about seven to eight blind Christians attending his house meetings. They lived a long distance from Yuan but near to one another, so Yuan suggested, 'Since it's not so convenient for you to move around, why don't we meet at one of your homes?' Wang DeMing offered to open up his house for meetings, and from then on Yuan travelled for an hour each week to lead a meeting at DeMing's. The meetings were greatly blessed by the Lord and grew from seven to about forty.

After the completion of his parole, the number of worshippers meeting at Yuan's house increased. Now the congregation had grown to about 300 and they met in three separate services, each one hundred strong. It was the largest house church among the one hundred or more house churches in Beijing, and so was noticed by the government. But Yuan was not afraid. He said, 'God brought me out of prison to serve Him. I'll serve Him as long as I live. Pastors can be arrested, but the Word of God cannot be bound.'

Yuan had to attend to many visitors and reply to many letters every day. Believers visited or wrote to him to ask for books or direction for their ministry. Some believers brought their unbelieving family members and friends so that Yuan could share the gospel with them. He also gave them gospel tracts.

He believed that the Book of Acts was the blueprint for the church, and said jokingly that a person would know how to manage the church after reading the Book of Acts one hundred times. He urged the churches to return to the model of the apostolic church as recorded in that book. He said, 'In this most unique period of Chinese Church history, the only model was the model house church. If you want to register as an official organisation, you're going the wrong way. Official organisations in China must come under the leadership of the Communist Party. If the Church accepts the leadership of the Communist Party, Christ is no longer the Head.'

Note

1. Of course, now he would be regarded as a fellow citizen.

Chapter 22

Friendship with Wang MingDao in the Latter Part of His Life

At the end of 1989, Yuan received his identity card and his Chinese citizenship was reinstated. Shortly afterwards, his identity card was in use – he went off to Shanghai to meet his old friend Wang MingDao. He was to have stayed with Chen BenWei, whose mother had been baptised in Yuan's Gospel Hall. Chen BenWei had graduated from Furen University and had taught classical Chinese in a secondary school before working in Xiaoqun Christian Bookshop. The two men had been friends for decades. When Chen BenWei met Yuan at the railway station, he said, 'Brother Yuan, there's a change of plan. Wang MingDao wept when he read your letter and found out that you were coming. He insisted that you and your wife stay at his place.' He said to HuiZhen, 'Mrs Wang spoke highly of you. She said that it was really the work of God that a woman as pretty as you would wait for Yuan for so many years.' So they made their to Wang MingDao's house with all their luggage.

When they arrived at his house, Mrs Wang supported her husband to the door. Wang MingDao said to Yuan, 'Yuan, I can no longer see you, oh, my brother.' He felt Yuan with his hands as he spoke. All of them wept. Yuan and his wife stayed with them for four days. They told each other about their lives over these past twenty years and encouraged each other. Wang MingDao had almost gone blind and deaf, so he spoke very loudly. He was also in poor health and sometimes he was unclear in what he said. Mrs Wang's memory was better than her husband's.

Wang MingDao told Yuan that his son, Wang TianDuo, had been baptised as a child. TianDuo was a respectful son, who came home and had dinner with his parents twice a week. On one of these visits, over dinner, Yuan asked TianDuo, 'We're old now. How is your faith?' TianDuo was silent at first but then he said, 'It's a long story. I'm living a good, secure life now. But look at my father: he suffered all these years because of his belief in Jesus and his ministry.' Later, he said that the Bible was unreliable and unscientific, especially the Book of Genesis. Nevertheless, Yuan still believed that TianDuo would return to his faith one day. He was a prodigal son, but he was still a son. One day, he would return.

The focus of MingDao and Yuan's conversation was the eleven leaders who had refused to join the Three-Self Movement. Some of them had given in when they had been threatened with arrest, some had betrayed others in the prison in order to obtain early release, and some had been brainwashed in the prison and had joined the Three-Self Movement after their release. The two men became very distressed when they talked about this. They had vowed before the Lord, but not all of them had persevered to the end. The one who had disappointed MingDao the most was Peng HongLiang who had been a young man at the time, ten years younger than Yuan. He had tried to imitate Wang MingDao in his gestures and preaching tone and had been known as 'the little Wang MingDao'. HongLiang had been the one who had suggested that Yuan send postcards to the other leaders to arrange a meeting. After he had been arrested, he had pushed all the blame onto Yuan, but Yuan had not mentioned his name when he was interrogated. As a result, HongLiang had been the earliest among them to be released, having spent only one year in prison. But God cannot be mocked. A man reaps what he sows. Even in prison, he used betrayal and blame-shifting to obtain an early release. But soon after his release, in 1962, he passed away. Someone had seen him on Dongda Bridge half paralysed, dragging his feet and speaking unclearly.

Another person about whom they spoke was Wu MuJia, who had been Yuan's neighbour. On the day of his arrest, he had been riding his bicycle in the alley. A policeman had stopped him and asked, 'What's your name?', handcuffing him when he identified himself. Afterwards, his house was searched. He had been a prisoner at the same prison as Yuan in the North-east. After he had been released, HuiZhen and Liu ShuJie visited him but he kept evading the topic of faith. Once HuiZhen gave him thirty dollars and a baked duck, but he told them, 'Please don't come to visit me any more. Every time you visit I have to explain it to a man with a long face. Please take all these back.' Later, he admitted that he had renounced his faith, 'Why should I believe in Christ? Karl Marx also renounced his original Christian faith. Why should I believe? I don't believe. That's it! I'm not lying. I'm glad that you have not divorced Yuan. Perhaps what you can do is bring him more books to reshape his thinking so that he can be released sooner. He's too stubborn.' On hearing this, HuiZhen was very distressed. MuJia's wife had passed away before his release, and he was grieving for her. He had also failed to get residency in Beijing, so he had stayed and worked where he was. He had said all this to HuiZhen in the presence of his eldest son, David. David asked him, 'What are you speaking up against?' MuJia had said, 'Christian faith. I'm no longer a Christian. I don't want to live a lie.' David had said, 'You're always betraying and falsely accusing others.' MuJia kept silent. HuiZhen left the thirty dollars there and went home. Afterwards, MuJia joined the Three-Self Movement. Mr Yin JiZeng, the Principal of the YanJing Theological Seminary, offered him a teaching position teaching Greek and he accepted. After he joined the Three-Self Movement, he had residency, a salary and a house. He did not inform his believers when he moved house. On one occasion, after he had preached in a Three-Self church on the topic of humility, Song TianZhen had written a letter to him, asking him, 'You preached very well. Why don't you speak about your failures? How you fell and denied the Lord. This testimony will help others.' MuJia said that he had been very grateful for TianZhen's letter for no one else had given him this reminder.

Later, MuJia visited Chen BenWei's mother, who was staying at Yuan's house at that time. He defended the words he had spoken to HuiZhen by saying, 'When I spoke like that, I was only speaking against theology.' Yet, he became a lecturer of theology.

Yuan said, 'Although MuJia and I suffered together, we've ended up on different paths.' On hearing this, MingDao shook his head, smiled wryly and sighed.

No one should be judged on appearances. The ultimate test is the fire of God's judgement. A person does not stand before God on the basis of his eloquence, but his faithfulness. Some have a good beginning but fail to persevere and end in disaster. Others who seem to be less gifted and have an insignificant beginning, nevertheless persevere to the end. Yuan always warned his co-workers, 'Don't despise anyone in the Lord, for you don't know what he'll be tomorrow. You don't know how God is going to lead him.'

Actually, before Yuan had visited MingDao in 1989, MingDao had been pondering the problems facing the House Church Movement in China. He had held a meeting at his house with eight co-workers and had even recorded the meeting on an audiocassette. Later, a man had invited HuiZhen to his house to listen to that cassette. HuiZhen asked him, 'Why don't you ask Yuan to come along?' He said, 'Yuan has only just been released from prison. He's lost touch with the world and cannot distinguish between the faithful and the deserter. You tell him the content after you've listened.' HuiZhen listened to what MingDao had said.

> 'There are two religious trends now. On the one hand there is a State-controlled Church, on the other hand there is the House Church Movement. The State-controlled Church has been oppressing the Christian faith through the Three-Self Movement. They are not one in heart and mind with me. I'm adamantly opposed to it. I'm on the Lord's side. But I regret that not many

are on the Lord's side. Many students and professionals have suffered because of their association with me. But those who do not bow to the government are really rare. There are only a few who have stood firm. There are only two brothers that give me the greatest comfort. One is Lin XianGao from Guangdong; the other is Yuan also from Guangdong. The others are mostly cowards that have broken my heart.'

Others in the meeting also gave a speech. One man said, 'We must not be manipulated by the Communist Party, neither should we manipulate others. We are preaching the Word of God and we've got nothing to fear.' At that time Wang MingDao's thinking was still very clear, and he did a lot of speaking. However, when Yuan and HuiZhen visited him in 1989, he was less lucid and kept repeating his thoughts.

Wang MingDao passed away in 1991. Yuan wrote an article in his memory entitled *In Remembrance of Mr Wang MingDao*.

Chapter 23

Interference

From the beginning of the Cultural Revolution, almost all the churches in China were closed down. Lots of Christian literature was burnt and all religious activities were stopped. Even the pastors of the Three-Self Movement were sent to the villages or put under corrective work orders. In 1979, following the economic reformation and the policy of openness to foreign countries, China's religious policy went through a series of changes. At the end of the 1970s, the government reinstated the religious policy which had been in existence before 1958 and abolished its former extreme left-wing policy. In June 1979, the Three-Self Movement had its first committee meeting since the Cultural Revolution and the Movement was officially restored. Former pastors in that Movement resumed their ministry. In February 1979, the first worship service since the Cultural Revolution took place at the Muen Church in Shanghai.

In the early part of 1980s, both the government and the Three-Self Movement accepted the existence of the House Church Movement. A leader from the Three-Self Movement even commented, 'Don't treat the House Church Movement as if it were alien. They are our brothers and sisters.' This acceptance was, however, short-lived. The leaders of the Three-Self Movement who had sent those who had refused to join them to prison began to tolerate the House Church Movement because during the Cultural Revolution they had also suffered at the hands of the government. This was a period when the true colours of the Three-Self leadership were exposed, and when God disciplined His wayward children. Some of them started to understand the sufferings of their brothers and sisters in Christ in the House Church Movement. But at this time also, the Three-Self Movement started to compete with the house churches.

However, in China, many religious matters were out of the control of the religious authorities. In 1982, the government issued its first official religious policy after the Cultural Revolution, entitled 'The Basic Viewpoint and Policy Concerning Religious Matters in Socialist China'. It was commonly known as Document 19. The policy promulgated that all religious sites had to be supervised by the government and were entrusted to religious organisations and clergymen. The House Church Movement was thus officially outlawed but steps were not taken to clamp down on it forcibly.

From 1979 to 1991 the Chinese House Church Movement flourished relatively free from the control of the government. By the early 1990s, the members of the House Church Movement far exceeded those of the Three-Self Movement. However, being more biblical, the House Church Movement could not win the favour of the government.

In these circumstances, the government issued the 'Notice on Follow-up Measures Dealing with Religious Matters', which was also known as Document 6. The document stressed the importance of overseeing religious matters and ruled that 'all religious sites should be registered and self-ordained pastors and propagation were banned.' The House Church Movement was explicitly outlawed.

Since 1991, some of the leaders of the House Church Movement have again been persecuted.

In February 1994, the State Council of China issued the 'Regulations of the Management of Religious Sites', also known as Document 145, which, as its name suggests, reinforced the ruling that all religious sites had to be registered.

In May 1994, in order to implement Document 145, the State Council of China issued the 'Methods of Registration of

Religious Sites', which listed the procedures for the registration of religious sites. The ruling required the House Church Movement to register but did not force it to come under the banner of any patriotic religious organisation. However, it contained an ambiguous statement requiring the presence of approved religious leaders which caused some house church leaders to fear that, once they had registered, the government might impose pastors from the Three-Self Movement on the churches and, for this reason, they refused to register. To counteract this, the government issued another decree making the registration compulsory. Any house churches which refused to register would have to stop meeting.

At the end of the summer of 1994, a Christian who was going abroad lent his house at No. 68, Nandouya Road, Zhaoyangmen, Eastern City, to Yuan. Yuan and HuiZhen moved there, but they continued to meet at White Pagoda Temple Street for worship. They decided to move to Nandouya Road because it was a quieter location and was better for guests. Moreover, once the bed and wardrobe had been removed, the meeting-point at White Pagoda Temple could accommodate another thirty members. The third reason for the move was that they could baptise believers in their new home.

A year later, the police started to create trouble for them. On 14 August 1995, some policemen came to Yuan's house and one of them said, 'You cannot live in this house any longer. There are too many people crowded into this house. And you have not signed a tenancy agreement. You must vacate the building as soon as possible. The "Fourth World Women's Convention" is due to take place, and so you must vacate it before this Friday. We'll come and check on that day.' He continued, 'Do you have any religious literature in your house?' Yuan replied, 'Yes, I do.' The policemen began to search the house. There was a lot of Christian literature in one of the rooms. Some of it was on the parapet, but most of it – a few hundred books – was kept in a cupboard. Yuan was afraid that the policeman might confiscate these books, which had been smuggled in by foreign Christians who had risked their lives. But the Holy Spirit had reminded him to be honest and none of the books inside the cupboard were discovered. They only confiscated the small amount of books on the parapet. After they left, Yuan said happily to HuiZhen, 'It is indeed worth telling the truth. The Lord will protect His own books.'

On Thursday night, the policemen came again. This time they were very harsh. Although it was already about 9.00 p.m., they summoned Yuan to see the police chief at the police station and, when they left, they took away some gospel tracts without issuing any statement of confiscation. At the police station Yuan said to the chief, 'Sir, we really cannot move before Friday. There are only the two of us old people at home. We can only move on Saturday when our children are off.' The chief backed down reluctantly. A policewoman, who was sitting next to the chief, asked Yuan, 'Do you know what the Three-Self Movement is?' He answered, 'Yes, I do.'

When he returned home, Yuan discovered that the police had sabotaged their telephone and this made him very angry. After the police left the telephone was no longer working. It was very obvious that the policemen were trying to put pressure on them through this. Yuan had to contact his family members and friends by public telephone in order to ask them to help them move house. The next day, when they had almost finished moving, the telephone was automatically repaired, without any one having reported the fault to the telecom bureau. This was another proof that the telephone had been sabotaged, and also indicated that they had been under surveillance.

Since his release in 1979, this was the first time he had encountered interference from the government for religious reasons. But this was only the beginning.

In 1996, Yuan received a visit from a government official who read a document which required him to register his house church. However, after he had scrutinised the regulations and discussed them with his co-workers, he decided not to register.

Mr Li, the Head of the Department of Religious Affairs in Western City, visited Yuan three times. He said to Yuan,

'Although this is not a formal religious site, it is nevertheless a religious site. Therefore, you must register.' But he did not press him further because he knew Yuan's influence over the House Church Movement and even religious bodies abroad. He asked Yuan to come to see him at his office a week later.

On the following Tuesday, Yuan went to Mr Li's office. They were very friendly towards Yuan and kept trying to persuade him of their policy. Yuan told him the outcome of his discussions with his co-workers, 'On 4 June we announced to our members that we would stop our meetings. We won't register because according to the second and sixth article of the Regulations on the Management of Religious Sites we do not qualify. We're meeting in my house, not a church building. Furthermore, I'm not an ordained pastor. We have neither charter nor funds. We won't register because we do not qualify.' Mr Li did not make any further comment because Yuan had said that they would stop meeting. He told Yuan that he intended to arrange a meeting of all the house church leaders in Western City which he wanted him to attend. But Yuan said, 'Since we're going to dissolve our house church, there is no need for me to attend the meeting.' Before he left, he left his name card and said, 'You can contact me at this phone number.' In this way he put an end to his tug of war with the government official for the time being.

Even though he had declared the house church disbanded, the believers continued to come, though the number initially decreased to about thirty. But the number soon increased again. After keeping them under observation for a while, Mr Li came back. This time he came prepared, bringing with him the police chief. One Sunday morning, while they were worshipping, Mr Li and the police chief shouted from outside, 'Ask Mr Yuan to come out.' The believers passed the message to Yuan who was still preaching. He stopped and went out to talk to them. The police chief said, 'Haven't we ask you to register? But you would not listen. All these people are meeting here illegally and you are blocking the traffic. You must stop now. Ask your members to clear this place.' Due to his hearing problem, he did not understand what the police chief had said, and he went back in and continued his preaching. When the police chief heard him preaching, he was very angry, and shouted even louder, 'Stop this now! I mean now! Ask Yuan to come out. The rest of you go home.' They chased away the old people while the police chief and Mr Li interrogated Yuan along with three young men. After checking their identity cards and asking them for their place of origin, they released the three young men, but continued talking to Yuan for twenty minutes. The police chief and Yuan argued until finally the police chief said, 'The older believers can continue to meet here, but the young men must meet in church. You must control the numbers. We will hold you responsible if the number increases again.'

Yuan defied the order and continued the meetings. Mr Li visited him a third time. Their discussion was very tense. Yuan said, 'The believers want to come to my house. I can't help it. Unless you seal my house and arrest me, they'll keep coming. As for me, my faith is above everything else. When the law of the country contradicts my faith, I can only obey God.' A woman was recording their conversation. Mr Li became very angry and said, 'Do you read your Bible? Haven't you read that you should obey the authority set above you? But you haven't been obeying the government. We can easily arrest you at any time. You must think about your family. They waited for you for more than twenty years. If you commit an offence again and are arrested, what will become of your wife?' Mr Li coupled persuasion with coercion. But Yuan still refused to register. Before he left, Mr Li said, 'Don't think we dare not touch you. I can easily order your arrest.' Yuan thought that they would come again to try to put pressure on him or even arrest him, but thank God, they did not. They did not come again to interrupt their meetings or force them to register.

When news about registration spread abroad, many foreigners were perplexed. They asked, 'Why not register? We are also required to register in our countries. The house church will be legal once it registers.' They did not understand that the legal system of the nation did not function well and the real intention of the government was to exert control over the house church under the guise of management.

Yuan told the believers, 'All of you must be prepared. We will meet as long as we can. If we are stopped one day, we'll move to other places. Meetings can be stopped but God's work cannot be stopped.'

Although the dispute regarding registration had blown over, Yuan's meeting was interrupted four more times.

The first time was during the handover of Hong Kong in 1997. The police station issued a notice banning meetings at Yuan's house for three days. The reason for this was that the nation's leaders were attending the handover ceremony in Hong Kong and, in order to ensure the security of Beijing, Yuan and his wife were taken away by car and lodged in an air-conditioned guest room near Yuan's house and the police station. They were taken to this guest room every morning and returned home every night. Two members of the force constantly accompanied them, but the police treated them well. Yuan and his wife spent the three days watching television. On Sunday 29 June the policeman came to fetch them earlier than usual in order to avoid being seen by the believers. There was a meeting on Tuesday night (1 July), so they did not take them home until late that night. All this indicated that the police were very familiar with the timing of the meetings at his house.

The second time was during the early autumn in September 1998. Representatives of three religious groups from the US were invited by President Jiang ZeMin to observe religious freedom in China. The government stopped Yuan's meeting for fear that the team might interview him. The police came to Yuan's house in Changping, Beijing, and said to him, 'Since the weather is so hot, why don't you study your Bible here?' They did not want to harm Yuan for fear of violating human rights so they only prevented him from leaving Changping. Yuan was later told that the visitors wanted to interview him but were prevented by the government.

Actually, on that day Yuan had arranged for a man by the name of Qiaozhi to come and preach at the house meeting at White Pagoda Temple Street. Qiaozhi did not know that

Yuan was prevented from attending the meeting. Knowing that Qiaozhi was coming, FuYin went to White Pagoda Temple Street at 10.00 a.m. When he arrived, he saw a policeman guarding the door, but he opened it and went in. The policeman followed him in and said to him, 'You'd better go home.' FuYin said, 'Why? This is my home.' The policeman said, 'Don't you know that today's meeting has been banned? You've got two choices. You can either go home or stay here. If you choose to stay here, you must inform us whenever you want to leave.' FuYin ignored him. He called his father in Changping. He spoke to AnHu, who was also living in Changping at that time. FuYin told her, 'White Pagoda Temple is being guarded by policemen.' AnHu said, 'There are also policemen here in Changping.' FuYin felt better when he knew that his parents were OK. At about noon, FuYin attempted to leave secretly in order to tell Qiaozhi and his friends not to come to the meeting, but a policeman followed him. FuYin pretended he was doing some shopping, and the policeman turned back. When he saw Qiaozhi and his three friends walking across the street, he beckoned to them. When they approached him, he said, 'The police are observing us. Go home now. There is no meeting today.' An interpreter interpreted for him. Meanwhile, two policemen approached them. One of them asked, 'What's going on?' FuYin replied, 'Nothing.' He asked again, 'What did you tell them?' FuYin answered, 'They're visitors asking for directions.' The policeman said to Qiaozhi, 'Show me your passport.' Qiaozhi took out a sweet and put it in his mouth. FuYin gestured to them. The four of them turned and walked away quickly. FuYin also turned and walked away. The police did not know whom to follow, but in the end they went after FuYin. When they caught up with him, they said, 'Go home immediately. You cannot walk around here.' Just before he entered his house, a young policeman approached him and said sternly, 'What did you say to them just now?' FuYin replied, 'I've told you. They were visitors asking for directions.' He said, 'No. You're not telling the truth.' FuYin replied, 'Say whatever you want to say. Weren't you there just now? Didn't you hear what they said?' FuYin became angry and continued, 'Can't I even talk freely in my own residential area?' An older policeman said, 'OK, forget it.' So they left it at that. When believers came, the policemen told them, 'There's no meeting today.' Some of them did not believe it. They asked, 'Why is there no meeting?' One of the policemen answered, 'Yuan is sick. You'd better leave.'

The third time was during the Fifteenth People's Congress. Yuan was forced to stop meeting for two weeks and was put under house arrest in Changping for that time.

The fourth time was when President Clinton visited Beijing. He was accompanied by more than two thousand reporters, and the government was afraid that the reporters might interview Yuan, so they stopped his meetings. Yuan said, 'Bill Clinton is a president. I'm only a commoner. He won't know me, and I don't know him. What has his visit got to do with me?' The government official replied, 'There are many reporters following President Clinton. They might interview you. Therefore, as long as President Clinton is in Beijing, you cannot hold meetings.' Yuan was furious, he said, 'Bill Clinton is your guest. I've not invited him over. You should take care of your guest, not confine me.' Finally, the government sent policemen to put Yuan under house arrest in Changping and ordered him to write a notice saying that the meeting was cancelled because he was sick. Yuan said, 'We Christians don't lie. I won't write a note.' The policemen blocked the road and dismissed the believers by saying that Yuan was sick.

Apart from these few incidents, Yuan was frequently summoned to the police station for interrogation about the matter of distributing Christian literature and the large number of believers meeting at his house. On 1 August 1998, Yuan rented a swimming pool in a factory in Beijing for two hours for the baptism of 316 people and again he was summoned to the police station. He said, 'I've done nothing wrong. I was only moving around in the swimming pool and did not block the traffic or cause any social unrest.' The policeman said, 'Religious activities can only be carried out in religious buildings.' Yuan said, 'This is beyond the bounds of the Religious Affairs Bureau. You're only responsible for ensuring that we remain patriotic. This is our business.' The policeman was furious. He warned, 'If you do that again, you will suffer the consequences.' Yuan decided to baptise his believers further away in future. The policeman reminded Yuan, '1999 is an important year. It's the handover of Macau and the tenth anniversary of the 4 June Democratic Movement. You'd better be prepared.' Yuan said, 'I know what you mean. You want to stop our meetings again. Actually, this is against the Constitution that guarantees freedom of religion. I'll serve the Lord as long as I live. I'm accountable to Him.'

Chapter 24

Contacts with Foreigners

In 1994 Dr Billy Graham visited Yuan and preached at his house. The purpose of Dr Graham's visit was to try and bring reconciliation between the house churches and the Three-Self churches. Three days before Dr Graham's arrival, Yuan had a fall when he was catching a bus to a meeting-point and suffered a blow to his forehead, which made him faint on the spot. Someone supported him by the roadside, enabling him to sit up and, after a while, he managed to stagger home. For a while he lost his ability to speak and his family were very anxious. They sterilised his wound with salt water and consulted the doctor over the phone. After observing him for twenty-four hours they were relieved to discover he was OK. When Dr Graham arrived three days later, his face was still badly bruised and he had to wear sunglasses when he was out.

When they were having their lunch together, Yuan sat beside Billy Graham's second son, who was the head of an organisation by the name of East Gates Ministry. He asked Yuan, 'The Three-Self churches are also doing a lot of good work. They print the Bible, spread the gospel and lead people to Christ. Why can't you co-operate with them? Shouldn't we Christians love even our enemies?' Yuan said, 'I'm afraid you've been deceived by their propaganda.' It is indeed very difficult for foreigners to understand the complicated religious situation in China.

At the beginning of every February in the USA Christian leaders from all walks of life from all over the world are invited to a prayer breakfast. As the White House's adviser on religious affairs at that time Dr Graham was in charge of the guest list. The Americans recognised Yuan from Beijing, Lin XianGao from Guangdong and Li TianEn from Shanghai as the three most prominent leaders of the House Church Movement and their names were included in the guest list for the prayer breakfast in February 1995. Leaders from the Three-Self Movement were also invited. After he had received the invitation, Yuan sought the Lord's direction through prayer but he did not feel prompted to go. Mrs Graham was very hospitable, and had given him a private invitation to stay on for three days at their house after the prayer breakfast. Yuan wrote a long letter to Mrs Graham, explaining the four reasons why he felt unable to attend.

1. He did not think that the government would issue him a passport because, having imprisoned him for so long, they would be afraid that Yuan would speak badly about the government.

2. He did not want to associate himself with any form of religious activity which had political connotations. This was the reason why he refused to join the Three-Self Movement. As the prayer breakfast was arranged by the US government, he would not attend.

3. The leaders of the Three-Self Movement were also invited. There was no room for interaction between them and him.

4. His health did not allow him to travel long distances.

Mrs Graham replied to his letter and tried to persuade him not to miss this opportunity. She answered his points.

1. The invitation was from the President of the USA – the Chinese government would not put any obstacles in the way. If he made the application, there should not be any problem.

2. (She did not answer the second point.)

3. Yuan need not feel obliged to have any discussions with members of the Three-Self Movement.

4. They would arrange for him to rest in San Francisco before going on to Washington.

Dr and Mrs Graham and the US government were sincere in their invitation. Nevertheless, Yuan decided that he must obey the prompting of the Holy Spirit. In his letter to Mrs Graham, he said that he would have accepted the invitation if it had been from Mrs Graham but he could not accept an invitation from the US government. Actually, all three house church leaders who had been invited declined without prior discussion with one another. Many foreigners advised Yuan, 'If you go, you and your ministry will benefit greatly.' He replied, 'Of course I'll benefit if I go. But I'm not concerned about myself. I'm concerned about sharing Christ and Him crucified. Dr Graham wants the house churches and the Three-Self churches to live in harmony, but it is impossible. Foreigners think that we cannot reconcile with the Three-Self churches because of old wounds that have not healed. But this is not the case. We cannot co-operate with them because we are headed in different directions. The head of the house churches is Christ while the head of the Three-Self churches is the government. We make decisions not according to our own will, but through prayer and the prompting of the Holy Spirit. All we are concerned about is walking according to the will of God.'

Chapter 25

Yuan's Theology

Since his conversion at age eighteen, Yuan had never worked in any secular company but had always served the Lord full time. Endowed with the gift of evangelism, he was especially patient in sharing the gospel. His sole calling was the ministry of the gospel and he was so absorbed by it that, when he was preaching or sharing the gospel, he would skip his meals. But God kept him strong and healthy. He had a Charismatic background, but he was an ardent Evangelical in his theology. He studied theology, but did not have a diploma. He never wrote a book, but he shepherded numerous sheep. His ministry was characterised by his insistence on two principles: one was his refusal to join any organisation; the second was his insistence on the house church model.

Yuan always claimed to be non-denominational. He never joined any denomination, or organisation. He never received any salary as an employee. He co-operated with foreign churches, but was not under them. He believed that a pastor should be called and sent directly by the Lord, and should trust the Lord not a regular salary. He believed that Christians should be actively involved in social relief such as giving donations for flood victims and other charitable works, but should be involved on a personal basis not under the banner of the church. Equally, Christians should also express their commitment to their country individually as citizens, not under the banner of the church.

Yuan was convinced that the Three-Self Movement was no longer needed. At the beginning of the liberation of China, there had been a need to emphasise self-propagation, self-support and self-government but for the last fifty years churches had been self-supporting, self-governing and self-propagating. Therefore, the Three-Self Movement had now accomplished its task. Every movement was temporary. The continued existence of the Movement served no purpose other than to be a government tool to control Christianity in China. The Three-Self Movement had no further contribution to make to the Church, for the Church only needed the power and the work of the Holy Spirit. Many had been disappointed by the Movement and had gradually left it. Its future was bleak. Though it was backed by political power, it was corrupt. It had a form of godliness, but lacked substance. According to the Bible, it was wood, hay and straw. It appeared to be bustling with life, but in fact it was only a useless human organisation. It matched Revelation's description of the church of Laodicea. It appeared to be rich, but was actually poor and naked. Worse still, they had left Jesus standing outside the door.

In spite of attempts to remould his thinking in prison for more than two decades, Yuan's stance on the separation between Church and State had not changed. The Religious Affairs Bureau claimed that it only focused on cultivating patriotism among Christians and would not tamper with the internal affairs of the churches. But this was a lie. Even though it promised not to control the Church, as emperors in the past had done, it actually exerted its control on almost every aspect of the churches' internal affairs. China had not implemented its stated religious policy and was still far away from true freedom of religion. It was indeed the obligation of Christians to love their nation, obey the laws and pay taxes, but if the laws of the country contradicted the commands of God, they should obey God, not human authority. Yuan expressed this view clearly on many occasions. He said, 'Actually, we are not super-political. But we hold to a principle. Pastors should focus on the ministry of the Word and prayer.'

Yuan held the view that the Apostles' Creed was the foundation of Christian faith, believing that it set out the criteria both for faith and for discerning heresy. On many occasions he used the Apostles' Creed to argue forcibly against liberal doctrines.

In the early stages of his ministry his theology was influenced by the Far East Mission with whom he had studied. Initially, he believed that it was possible for Christians to fall from grace and lose their salvation. He did not hold to the teaching: once saved, always saved. This was what he was taught in class and he believed it. Later, when his theology was maturing and being tested against experience, he found this doctrine problematic and he began to reconsider, eventually changing his position. He believed that a born-again Christian had a new life. If he sinned, his conscience would be uneasy. If he continued to sin, God would discipline him, so that he would repent and not fall away. This is a thorny theological question, but Yuan believed that salvation was dependent on God not man.

At the Far East Theological Seminary, four doctrines were stressed: regeneration, sanctification, divine healing and the second coming. Yuan believed that a changed life was the main indication of whether or not a person had been born again. According to the promise of the Bible, sanctification follows regeneration. Through the empowering of the Holy Spirit, a Christian is set apart by God for victorious Christian living. The baptism of the Holy Spirit is received through being filled by the Holy Spirit. This is the second grace. Sanctification does not mean sinless perfection, but it promises power to overcome sins. There is still the possibility of failure, but it is possible through the Holy Spirit to overcome the flesh. It is not that there is no longer a possibility to sin, but there is a possibility not to sin. A person is sanctified positionally when he is born again, but he has yet to work it out in his life. In regeneration, one is declared righteous, but in sanctification, one becomes righteous.

Yuan believed in the doctrine of original and actual sins. Original sin was inherited while actual sins were committed by each individual.

Yuan believed that the understanding of the doctrine of the Trinity was foundational to the Christian faith. He considered anyone who denied this doctrine to be a heretic. Yuan also believed in the tripartite division of man, and in this he was obviously influenced by theological trends in China in the 1950s.

In his preaching, he often taught young Christians how to discern the will of God. He believed that there were three aspects to this discerning.

1. The prompting of the Holy Spirit. A Christian should learn to differentiate the moving of the Holy Spirit from the promptings of self or Satan.

2. The prompting of the Spirit is always in accordance with Scripture. Everything that is not in accordance with the Scripture is not the will of God.

3. The indication of circumstances. If circumstances do not allow something to happen, it indicates that the time is not yet right, and a person needs to wait.

Anything that is the will of God would pass these three tests.

In his preaching, Yuan constantly alluded to the cross and its meaning, particularly emphasising the salvation that it brought, and the life of bearing the cross and following the Lord. We tend to want to escape from bearing the cross and suffering but Christians are called to bear their cross and follow the Lord throughout their lives. The cross was the sign of shame and suffering. Without the cross, there would be no glory for one day it would be exchanged for the crown of righteousness. Therefore, Yuan exhorted believers to bear their crosses willingly. He told them that their present difficulties were nothing compared to the glory that they would one day receive. When people would ask him, 'You've spent so many years in prison. Was it difficult?' he would say, 'It's nothing in comparison with the cross of Christ.' Through God's grace, he despised his own sufferings and was willing to suffer and even be martyred for the Lord. His ability to focus on the cross of Christ enabled him not to become bogged down by his own sufferings. Many prisoners committed suicide, but this had never crossed Yuan's mind. He believed that the Lord was in control of everything and his sufferings were insignificant in comparison with the Lord's.

The problems of church growth are crucial whether in the initial stages of the liberation of China or now. Yuan had always believed in self-supporting and self-propagating churches, and that is why he never joined any denomination. Although small in scale, his ministry was nevertheless contextualised. He built his ministry gradually, in the beginning working part time to earn his livelihood while serving the Lord. He was quite optimistic about the future. He believed that the Church flourished in the midst of afflictions and persecutions. The number of believers increased as the persecution increased. In 1900, many missionaries were killed in China, as were many Christians, especially in Shanxi. Through great persecution, the Christian population had indeed grown. According to statistics from Hong Kong, 9 per cent of the Chinese population were Christians. This statistic might appear a bit exaggerated, and because the House Church Movement refused to disclose the number of believers connected with it, it could never be confirmed. Whatever the statistic, the members of the House Church Movement far exceeded those of the Three-Self Movement. Some people asked Yuan, 'Has the religious policy been loosened or tightened?' Yuan replied, 'I don't care if it has been loosened or tightened. We've got to continue to do the work of God. Just as in the time of the apostles, the authority of hell can never prevail over the Church. Then, as now, the preaching of the gospel is attested by signs and wonders. The flame of revival is spreading all over the world, including China.'

Yuan held firmly to the promise of God. He often exhorted his co-workers, 'Many are actually prepared to receive the gospel, we need to be bold enough to share it. Modern people have a void in their hearts which can only be filled by the Lord. They are receptive to the gospel. By spreading the gospel, we can hasten the return of Christ. Therefore, we must grasp every opportunity we can. When the number of the redeemed is full, the Lord will return.' But Yuan always reminded them to rely on the Lord, not on might or power. He said, 'The Church lacks the gifts of the Holy Spirit. If we exercise the spiritual gifts in our ministry, the results will be great. Therefore, we must pursue the filling of the Spirit and the spiritual gifts on the one hand, and bear the fruit of the Spirit on the other.'

In the area of church organisation, Yuan believed that local churches should be autonomous and independent. There was no such thing as organisational unity in the Bible. Organisational unity was man-made. The Book of Revelation referred to the seven churches in Asia Minor. John did not write to the bishop of the entire region of Asia Minor. Those churches were autonomous and independent. There should be ties between churches in spiritual and material matters, but they should be independent administratively. During the great flood in Anhui, such a relationship was well illustrated. Various churches in Beijing donated aid to the victims and helped with the relief work. This was appropriate. Churches could invite pastors from other churches to preach. But there was no need for organisational alliance. The Bible did not mention headquarters, branches, mother churches or daughter churches. All churches were equal. God's plan was universal. Chinese churches were part of His universal plan.

Regarding the House Church Movement Yuan believed that the strength of the house meetings was enormous. 'House churches are blossoming everywhere' was his slogan. He believed that when each Christian home was a sentry for the gospel, the gospel would spread more rapidly. He emphasised repeatedly that there should be no organisation. The Church was neither an earthly organisation nor a civilian body. In the 1940s to 1950s, Yuan and MingDao did not discuss church affairs, for they were all independent, and in fact they did not meet very often. Sometimes, MingDao would give some of his books to Yuan and preach in his church. They only had a loose partnership and remained independent.

Yuan believed that miracles still happen today. He had experienced miracles in his own life and had also cast out demons from people. He had even been miraculously healed by the Lord. After his conversion, he never took any medicine because he believed that God could heal him. Thank God, he never fell ill in prison. He was just like the Israelites whose clothes had not worn out, the Bible tells us, even after forty years in the wilderness.

In March 1998, he was hospitalised for the first time since his conversion. He was suffering from inflammation of the tear glands and his eyes were enflamed and bloodshot, and kept filling with tears. When he was taken onto the ward, he said, 'This place is too messy. I want to go home.' HuiZhen persuaded him to stay, saying, 'But you're so sick.' After surgery, he came down with a cold and fever and had to be transferred from ophthalmology to the general ward where he underwent a thorough medical check-up. The nurse took bloodtests every day. He was very unhappy about this and refused to allow himself to be vaccinated. He said, 'I don't want an injection. I'll recover soon.' Afterwards, he prayed loudly in the ward and was covered with perspiration. He felt that the Lord had healed him and wanted to be discharged immediately. His family persuaded him to stay two more days. But he said, 'God has healed me. Why won't you believe?' He kept insisting until eventually they had to give in. When he was paying, he was shocked by the medical fees. He said to HuiZhen, 'You see, didn't I say that I didn't want to be admitted? But you wouldn't listen. Now we've got to pay so much for treatment that has hardly done any good. Take this as a lesson.' Before he left, the doctor had one of his family sign a disclaimer which read, 'The doctor did not approve the discharge, but it was insisted on by the patient. The hospital is not liable for any adverse conse-quences.' AnHu signed the agreement on behalf of her father. Before he left, the doctor prescribed him some medicine worth a few hundred dollars. He said, 'No need. I've already recovered.' He had indeed truly recovered. The time in hospital had been his only opportunity to talk to his children at length and find out about their lives throughout the years of his absence, and how they had ended up in their present jobs.

In 1998 Yuan's health began to deteriorate and he finally had to give in and begin to take medicine. Prior to that, he had insisted on not taking any medicine when he was ill. In the beginning, he refused to take medicine even when urged by his family but, later, his co-workers successfully persuaded him. But every time he took medicine he would say, 'Actually I don't need this medicine. I've done without medicine for decades and God has looked after me. Now you're treating me like a prince. But I'll back down just to obey the body of Christ, not to be healed.'

In the early part of the 1990s, the Charismatic Movement impacted the Chinese Church. Yuan was ardently opposed to some of the Charismatics' teaching, but he did not rule out the work of the Holy Spirit. He said, 'We need the Holy Spirit. I received the Holy Spirit when I was nineteen. We should seek the Spirit by faith.' He believed that being born again and being filled with the Spirit were two different outworkings of the Holy Spirit. Being filled with the Holy Spirit led to different experiences: some laughed, some wept, some went hot and cold, some felt electric shocks going through their body, some clapped, some jumped in the air and some rolled on the floor. From his own experience, he believed that when the Spirit of the Lord of Hosts filled an insignificant man, something spectacular was bound to happen. Only a few people did not feel anything. But as in being born again, when it came to being filled with the Spirit faith was more important than feeling.

Yuan would sometimes preach on the topic of speaking in tongues in his meetings. He said that there were three kinds of tongues in the Bible. The first was the ability to speak in foreign languages so that native speakers of that language could understand without any interpretation. The second was a spiritual gift as listed in 1 Corinthians 12. The third was praying and singing in the Spirit as recorded in 1 Corinthians 14. During worship services, the practice of speaking in tongues was forbidden if there was no interpreter. Even if there was an interpreter, the aim of the gift was to edify the church. It was preferable to use the gift in private.

Yuan often spoke out against the excesses of the Charismatic Movement. According to Yuan, Li ChangShou was also critical of the Charismatics. He believed that the Charismatic Movement was soulish and fleshy, and neglected spiritual growth. Christians should pursue truth and knowledge, not outward manifestations. In spite of the heretical thoughts of Li ChangShou, such as his doubting of the doctrine of the Trinity, and his belief that Jesus was created, Yuan agreed with him on the subject of the Charismatic Movement. Some accused Yuan of having a Charismatic bias but he said, 'I don't belong to any denomination. I don't speak in tongues. I don't think that a person has to speak in tongues in order to be saved. As Christians we should be balanced. We should pursue being filled with the Holy Spirit, but not in the way the Charismatics do. We should be biblically balanced.' He was accused of being a Charismatic because some Charismatic leaders from Norway had visited him. Yuan said, 'My door is open to all. As long as you believe in the Apostles' Creed, you're welcome. But it doesn't mean that I must adopt your views.' Yuan felt that the Charismatics had their strengths and their contribution to make, but they placed too much emphasis on speaking in tongues and divine healing. He told the believers, 'We shouldn't throw the baby out with the bath water. We shouldn't allow our fear of Charismatic excesses to stop us wanting to be filled with the Holy Spirit. We should seek the gifts and the cleansing work of the Holy Spirit. We need to emphasise maturity, cleansing and power from the Holy Spirit.'

Yuan emphasised mutual support and encouragement between believers. He allotted a considerable amount of time in his meetings for the sharing of testimonies. After the service, believers would stay for fellowship. Yuan said, 'As Christians we belong to a family. Therefore, we should have fellowship with one another. If we don't talk to one another, can we claim that we are a family?'

Chapter 26

Take My Hand,
Lead Me On

Yuan was saved at age eighteen, and dedicated his life for full-time ministry at age twenty. After four years of theological training, he embarked on his ministry which was to span four decades. The first half of his ministry began with his graduation from the theological seminary and ended with his arrest (1938–58). The second half began in 1980 and continues until today. These two periods are separated by almost twenty-two years. His adulthood could be summarised by two words, 'ministry' and 'imprisonment'.

Yuan's life spanned the most important eras of the evangelisation of China. He was born in the era of the first wave of the revival of evangelism in China. In this era, he received the gospel and the call to spread the gospel. He also completed his first twenty years of ministry. In the era of great persecution, he held fast to the testimony of Christ and spent his best years in prison. After his release, he continued to be used greatly by the Lord. He became a great warrior of the gospel in the second wave of the revival of evangelism in China after 1980. He thought that he had wasted twenty years in prison, but God accomplished a greater feat in this second half of his ministry than even what he had accomplished in the first half.

When he was in the prison, a Scripture verse was constantly ringing in his ears,

*'Now I want you to know, brothers, that what has happened
to me has really served to advance the gospel.'*
(Philippians 1:12)

At that time he believed by simple faith that everything that
happened to him was part of God's wonderful plan for his
life. He thought that God wanted him to glorify Him by
being a martyr. Never did he imagine that God wanted him
to be a warrior for the gospel for another two decades. His
sufferings also became a blessing in disguise for the many
Chinese who came to know Christ through him. His life was
an integral part of the development of the modern history of
the Chinese Church.

We have seen the trail of history and the hand of God in
Yuan's life. In God's plan, we all have the same objective: to
witness for the Lord, in different times and with different
methods. But we are all witnessing to the same God. Before
God, all the great figures of history become insignificant. The
righteousness of God is established in heaven, and His works
are revealed on earth. Today, Liberal theology has already
been swallowed up by the tide of history and rendered
obsolete. Evangelical theology is on the rise. This is the work
of God. Chinese Christian workers have been faithful
witnesses for God. Their fervent and firm spirit in defending
the truth has built a strong foundation for Christianity in
China.

What God values is neither talent nor human wisdom. He
values the faithfulness of His children. The servants who
have been used greatly by the Lord have given their lives as
living sacrifices and have become channels through which
God blesses all nations. The servants of God are used greatly
by the Lord but not because of their superior intelligence or
knowledge. They are used greatly by the Lord because they
have the presence of His Spirit whose light exposes all their
blemishes and weaknesses so that they can avoid the
mistakes caused by their weaknesses.

Yuan was well aware of his weaknesses. He often talked
with his co-workers about them and asked them to help him
overcome them. His weaknesses included:

1. bad temper,
2. carelessness,
3. poor memory and analytic ability, and
4. an inability to express himself in a vivid way.

Nevertheless, God used him greatly. For God valued his availability, not his abilities. Yuan never tired of sharing the gospel with everyone who visited him. He spent time before and after every meeting showing concern for newcomers. His co-workers would say to him, 'Mr Yuan, you'd better take a rest. We'll look after the newcomers. It's not a big deal.' Yuan said, 'No work is insignificant in the sight of God. My life is full of these seemingly insignificant things.' He gave his life as a living sacrifice to the Lord and served Him faithfully in His temple.

Throughout his life Yuan's health has always been poor, especially in his childhood and youth. But God has kept him and granted him faith and incredible vitality for ministry. God also preserved his health through his two decades of imprisonment, when there was no medical care. It was incredible that his health actually improved after his imprisonment. Yuan always told the believers, 'I'll serve the Lord as long as I'm able. Who knows when the Lord will take me back to Him or come again? To be blameless before Him is all I ask. If I had not believed in Him, I wouldn't have been so blessed. It is the Lord who takes my hand and leads me in my life.' Yuan always said that he was unworthy to receive a reward or a crown because Revelation says that crowns would be placed before the Lord. He knew that all things were by the grace of God. He strove to be a faithful and wise servant, and live in the grace of God.

God has held Yuan's hand and led him through his life. In the same way He will take the hand of each of His children and lead them on His delightful path.

Epilogue

The main purpose for writing this book was to get to know a man – an ordinary man who nevertheless magnified the grace of God, a man who gave himself willingly as a living sacrifice, a man who gave his entire life to serve God as His vessel.

Another purpose for writing this book was to record the history of a crucial period in the development of the history of the Church in China.

Every era in history has its own God-given emphases, as well as its own blind spots. The emphasis of Christianity in this century in the evangelisation of China has been focused on the identification of the gospel with the indigenous culture and the alignment of the relationship between State and Church. While serving as the God-given commissions of the time, these two issues have also exposed the era's blind spots. What is God's perspective of this period of human history? This is the question with which the evangelisation of China in the twentieth century inevitably leaves us. It is a major challenge for the Chinese Christian in the twenty-first century.

In the same way, a man dedicated to God also reflects his sense of mission as well as his blind spots through his life. God's servants, though they love God and willingly give all to Him, are none the less imperfect. We can neither boast nor become absorbed in self-pity before God, because He has loved us and bestows us with mercy and truth. Our responsibility is to respond to His love.

With God's presence, a seemingly insignificant life becomes uniquely significant; with God's presence, human history radiates with His glory.

History does not develop in a single linear line. God is the only Lord of history. We may not be able to discern His will in the outworking of history. Likewise, life is a mystery. No one has the final say about another person's life. For to make such a judgement makes us Lord.

In this book I have simply tried to narrate God's guidance of an ordinary life, and to describe how this one man witnessed for the Lord in his generation. The author makes no attempt to make any judgement on any man or history but desires that the readers will be touched by this man who gave his life on the altar, and that it will be a source of inspiration for others to do likewise.

May more Chinese be blessed in the twenty-first century.

Open Doors Addresses

Open Doors
PO Box 53
Seaforth
New South Wales 2092
AUSTRALIA

Missao Portas Abertas
CP 45371
Vila Mariana
CEP 04010-970
Sao Paulo
BRAZIL

Open Doors
PO Box 597
Streetsville, ON
L5M 2C1
CANADA

Åbne Døre
PO Box 171
DK-6900 Skjern
DENMARK

Portes Ouvertes
BP 139
67833 TANNERIES
cedex (Strasbourg)
FRANCE

Offene Grenzen
Postfach 2010
D-38718 Seesen
GERMANY

Porte Aperte
CP45
37063 Isola Della Scala, VR
ITALY

Open Doors
Hyerim Presbyterian Church
Street No. 403
Sungne 3-dong
Kandong-gu #134-033
Seoul
KOREA

Open Doors
PO Box 47
3850 AA Ermelo
THE NETHERLANDS

Open Doors
PO Box 27-630
Mt Roskill
Auckland 1030
NEW ZEALAND

Åpne Dører
Boks 4698 Grim
N-4673 Kristiansand
NORWAY

Open Doors
PO Box 1573-1155
QCCPO Main
1100 Quezon City
PHILIPPINES

Open Doors
Raffles City Post Office
PO Box 150
SINGAPORE 911705
Republic of Singapore

Open Doors
Box 990099
Kibler Park 2053
Johannesburg
SOUTH AFRICA

Puertas Abiertas
Apartado 578
28850 Torrejon de Ardoz
Madrid
SPAIN

Portes Ouvertes
Case Postale 267
CH-1008 Prilly
Lausanne
SWITZERLAND

Open Doors
PO Box 6
Witney
Oxon OX29 7SP
UNITED KINGDOM

Open Doors
PO Box 27001
Santa Ana, CA 92799
USA

If you have enjoyed this book and would like to help us to send a copy of it and many other titles to needy pastors in the **Third World**, please write for further information or send your gift to:

Sovereign World Trust
PO Box 777, Tonbridge
Kent TN11 0ZS
United Kingdom

or to the **'Sovereign World'** distributor in your country.

Visit our website at **www.sovereign-world.org**
for a full range of Sovereign World books.